TRACING YOUR ROYAL MARINE ANCESTORS

TRACING YOUR ROYAL MARINE ANCESTORS

RICHARD BROOKS
and
MATTHEW LITTLE

*Published in association with
the Royal Marines Museum*

Pen & Sword
FAMILY HISTORY

First published in Great Britain in 2008 by
Pen & Sword Family History
an imprint of
Pen & Sword Books Ltd
47 Church Street
Barnsley
South Yorkshire
S70 2AS

ISBN 978 1 84415869 0

Typeset in Palatino by
Phoenix Typesetting, Auldgirth, Dumfriesshire

Printed and bound in England by
CPI UK

Pen & Sword Books Ltd incorporates the imprints of Pen & Sword Aviation,
Pen & Sword Maritime, Pen & Sword Military, Wharncliffe Local History,
Pen & Sword Select, Pen & Sword Military Classics and Leo Cooper.

For a complete list of Pen & Sword titles please contact
PEN & SWORD BOOKS LIMITED
47 Church Street, Barnsley, South Yorkshire, S70 2AS, England
E-mail: enquiries@pen-and-sword.co.uk
Website: www.pen-and-sword.co.uk

Front Cover, from left to right:
1) Studio photograph of Bugler 'Sticks' Burnett RMLI, HMS *Suffolk* (1917–1918)
2) Combined Operations Organization insignia (1942–1946)
3) General Service Medal (1962) with bar for Radfan campaign (1967)
4) Royal Marine sentinel of 1805 (Charles Stadden)
5) Royal Marine other ranks cap badge 1953 to date
6) Coloured postcard showing Barrack Gate, Forton Barracks, Gosport *c.*1910

CONTENTS

'There is no fighting force under the Crown less understood than the marines. Few trouble themselves to know more than that they are useful. Why they exist or why they are useful are not questions which attract attention.'

(*Army & Navy Gazette* 7 February 1874)

PREFACE

The Royal Marines (RM) are at once one of the most prestigious and most perplexing parts of the Armed Forces of the British Crown. Although clearly soldiers and holding military rank, marines have been part of the Royal Navy (RN) for over 250 years, providing between a tenth and a quarter of its manpower. Tracing descent from the Duke of York and Albany's Maritime Regiment of Foot of 1664, they were disbanded five times before permanent establishment in 1755. Then organized into Grand Divisions wearing red or blue, they are now organized as commandos and mostly wear green, except in the band service. Royal Marines officers appear in both the Army and Navy Lists, and at one time had their own list of officers of the Marine Forces. Not until 1802, however, did they receive the distinction 'Royal'. For over three centuries marines have played an essential part in the Royal Navy's most outstanding achievements, from the capture of Gibraltar in 1704 to the final frustration of French invasion plans at Trafalgar (when a Royal Marine sergeant helped carry the dying Nelson below), to the reconquest of the Falkland Islands in 1982.

The existence of a single unified body of marines is of more than incidental interest to the family historian. The large numbers of men serving as marines at different times makes the Corps a statistically more significant source of military ancestors than any infantry or cavalry regiment. Except during the wartime emergencies of 1914–18 and 1939–45, army regiments never exceeded a couple of thousand men apiece. Marine strength, by contrast, hovered between 10,000 and 20,000 throughout the nineteenth century, with far higher numbers in wartime. Despite the Cold War 'peace dividend', there are still over 6,000 Royal Marines. Besides their numbers the interior economy of the marines as established in 1755 also made them more likely to appear in a family tree. Regular stays at divisional headquarters between periods at sea encouraged long-term relationships, denied to soldiers shipped overseas, for seven or twelve years at a time. Marines were family men, and their sons followed them into the Corps, inspiring the claim that 'they don't recruit marines, they breed 'em'.

The position of these soldiers at sea has not always been easy to comprehend. Sir John Colomb, a Royal Marine Artillery (RMA) officer and Member of Parliament, described his old Corps in the 1880s as presenting 'a picture of confused anomalies and inconsistencies'. 'You see, chum,' said Private Henry Derry, a veteran of the 1840s and '50s, 'I can't separate we Joeys from the Jacks, nor the Jacks from we Joeys, so we get lost.' Naval officers took advantage of the confusion to steal the limelight: 'THE LAURELS WHICH YOU WIN', wrote an irate subaltern of the 1780s, 'OTHERS WEAR'. Historians have contributed towards the invisibility of the Corps. Christopher Lloyd's *The British Seaman* has a single index entry for marines, as if the story of the lower deck can be told without discussing the interaction between sailors and marines. John Keegan's *Battle at Sea* has none at all, despite the red jackets on its cover.

The sources available to family historians seeking a marine ancestor reflect the anomalous position of the Marine Corps within, but not of, the Royal Navy. Its possession since the mid-eighteenth century, of fixed headquarters in the navy's home ports at Chatham, Portsmouth and Plymouth has encouraged the survival of numerous classes of records. Army regiments had no fixed homes until the later 1800s. The routine of marine barrack life inspired the keeping of domestic records such as divisional registers of births, marriages and deaths. The monotony of service at sea encouraged officers and marines to keep personal diaries and notebooks, examples of which still find their way to the Royal Marines Museum.

This wealth of material is balanced by corresponding gaps. The nature of their service posed peculiar threats to the survival of marine records. HMS *Chichester*'s returns for February–July 1707 went down off the Scilly Isles with Admiral Sir Cloudesley Shovell. More banal accidents have taken their toll. Major Thomas Wybourne RM lost four volumes of his journal in the post. None of the surviving documents was kept for the benefit of genealogists. Colonel Lourenço Edye, the great historian of early marines, lamented the deficiencies of seventeenth-century records, 'which are either mutilated by the ravages of time or are deficient in the very essentials which render them so interesting to the modern student'. Divisional officers and Admiralty clerks would have been astonished to learn that anyone would ever look at their letters and returns again. Not only are official documents organized in an unhelpful manner, they are incomplete. The nineteenth and early twentieth centuries were richly documented, a situation since threatened by wartime economy paper, unstable electronic records and record retention policies driven by accountants rather than archivists.

The chronological and geographical spread of the services of the Royal Marines present particular difficulties for the researcher. The *Globe & Laurel*, the Corps journal and a prime reference for family historians, once commented, 'the story of the marines from beginning to end must approximate to a history of the British at war'. This work, therefore, avoids detailed operational narrative, inappropriate in a handbook aimed at genealogists with no special interest in naval or military history. Instead it concentrates on the context within which a marine ancestor might have served. The book falls into two main parts. Chapters 1 to 3 describe the purpose and evolution of the Royal Marines, how they were raised, paid, equipped, and sent to sea, and finally the types of operations in which they took part. Intended to be read as a narrative, these chapters are sub-divided into sections dealing with specific matters, for example landing craft, which can be referenced individually. Chapter 4 analyzes available records, explaining how to use them to trace the career of an individual marine. Researchers with a specific enquiry, for example concerning attestations, may go direct to the appropriate section of that chapter. Those requiring further information about particular aspects of Royal Marine history should consult the general histories in the Further Reading section and their bibliographies.

Note on military ranks

It will be helpful to remember the following about the military hierarchy, as implemented in the marine service:

1. Commissioned officers (in declining order of seniority)

- Colonels and lieutenant colonels might command a Grand Division at home, a battalion or Commando RM in the field (400–1,000 men), assisted by one or more majors. Known as 'field officers' they rarely went to sea.
- Captains might command a company ashore (50–100 men), or the marine detachment of a ship-of-the-line (74–100 guns), such as HMS *Victory*, with one or more lieutenants. Captains RM were called 'major' at sea.
- Lieutenants commanded half-companies and platoons (30–50 men), or the detachment of a frigate (28–46 guns) such as HMS *Trincomalee*, now preserved at Hartlepool.

2. Non-commissioned officers (NCOs)
These include sergeants, corporals, and (in the RMA) bombardiers. At one time NCOs included drummers. Sergeants and occasionally corporals might command the detachment of a small ship with fewer than twenty guns. They would then be known as the sergeant-major of marines regardless of the rank for which they drew pay. Colour sergeants appeared in the Corps in 1814, as a step up for deserving sergeants.

3. Other ranks

These are known as:

- Private until 1923, or gunner in the RMA.
- Marine since 1923.

References to 'marines', as opposed to 'seamen', appear without a capital letter. 'Marines' and 'Royal Marines' take a capital when used as proper nouns, for example as an individual's rank, or the title of the Corps.

Note on weights, measures and currency

These have suffered radical changes since the 1970s, after most of the events described in this book. Imperial measurements and pre-decimal currency have been used when appropriate, for example:

- Weights (e.g. of rations or projectiles) were usually quoted in pounds (lbs) equivalent to 454gm.
- Linear measurements (e.g. height of recruits or calibres of weapons) were given in yards (yds), feet (ft) and inches (ins). There were twelve inches (2.54cm) to a foot (30.48cm), and three feet to the yard (0.9144m).
- Money was specified in three units:
  Pounds (£)
  Shillings (s) at twenty to the pound, worth five new pence each.
  Pence (d) at twelve to the shilling, worth 0.42 new pence each.

Prices were expressed in all three, e.g. £5 3s 7d (£5.18p), or two, e.g. 2s 6d (12.5p), or one, e.g. 8d, or in words e.g. five shillings (25p). Luxury goods were priced in guineas worth £1 1s 0d, or £1.05 in modern currency.

ACKNOWLEDGEMENTS

The authors would like to acknowledge the support and assistance of the following:

The Trustees of the Royal Marines Museum, Eastney, Portsmouth, John Ambler, Major Mark Bentinck RM, Major Alistair Donald RM, Colonel Brian Edwards RM, Roy Inkersole and Captain Roy Swales RN.

Chapter 1

ORGANIZATION – WHAT IS A MARINE?

1.1 Function and purpose of a marine

Marines are soldiers raised and trained for service at sea. This broad statement has covered many tasks, for example shipboard security, naval gunnery or amphibious assault, which are sometimes mistaken for the true purpose of the Corps. Marines have two central functions in the British service:

1. To reinforce the personnel of the Royal Navy, acting as its first reserve.
2. To perform military tasks to which sailors may be unsuited.

Traditional maritime sources of naval manpower, the merchant and fishing fleets, were not always sufficient for these purposes. Enlistment of marines tapped alternative pools of manpower in agricultural or manufacturing districts, which otherwise contributed little to the Royal Navy. Many shipboard tasks required little ingrained seamanship. Marines were just as capable as sailors of hauling on a rope or walking round the capstan.

The crew of a warship requires a mixture of skills. The initiative and agility needed to work aloft in a sailing ship were quite different from the unthinking obedience and rigidity demanded by eighteenth- and early nineteenth-century military tactics. Captain Basil Hall RN contrasted the bearing of the two classes of naval personnel: Joe the marine looking as if he had swallowed a poker, Jolly Jack Tar rolling along as if constructed of springs and universal joints. Until the Continuous Service Act of 1853 seamen enlisted in the Royal Navy for one commission at a time. When their ship paid off they dispersed, losing any group cohesion they might have acquired. Permanently embodied marines added discipline to newly commissioned ships' crews, fresh from quayside grogshops. Modern sailors require no such stiffening, but the technical complexity of their calling seems unlikely to equip them for the military

1

aspects of naval work, for example patrolling disputed waterways in small boats.

Passing circumstance often obscures the underlying reasons for the existence of the Royal Marines. The Corps has a chameleon-like ability to refashion itself to avoid reduction or disbandment. When the Victorian navy no longer needed a disciplined reservoir of unskilled labour, Royal Marine Light Infantry (RMLI) became naval gunners. When missiles replaced guns, Royal Marine Commandos took up counter-insurgency and Arctic warfare. Today they provide the military component of Britain's Maritime Strike and Littoral Manoeuvre capability, alongside submarines, aviation assets and surface ships. These passing specialties, however expedient, are less an end in themselves than a means of fulfilling the basic function of the Corps, that is, to supplement the numbers and skills of the Royal Navy.

1.2 Evolution of the Corps 1664–2008

The history of the Royal Marines falls into three stages. Its beginnings were spasmodic and discontinuous for example between 1698 and 1702 or 1748 and 1755, while the Marine Invalids were of questionable value. The two centuries following 1755 were, by contrast, a period of administrative and geographical stability. Since the 1940s the Corps has once more undergone dramatic changes.

It is easy to view the evolution of the Royal Marines in Whig terms, commencing amidst Stuart muddle and corruption, progressing inexorably through Nelsonic heroism and Victorian orderliness to the cool professionalism of today. This would be misleading. Dynamic periods when the Corps acquired new roles and glory, such as the Napoleonic Wars, have always alternated with periods of complacency and neglect, as between the world wars. Most change resulted less from farsightedness than as a short-term response to present problems. The RMA arose from a squabble between Lord Nelson and some Royal Artillery (RA) subalterns, not a sudden appreciation of the importance of naval gunnery.

The health of the Corps at any time reflected the conditions of the day. The fly-by-night regiments of King William and Queen Anne were victims of post-revolutionary politics, following James II's overthrow in 1688, as well as administrative incapacity. A standing army was considered a threat to freedom, a regrettable necessity in wartime to be disbanded as soon as possible. It took the truly dreadful experiences of the War of Jenkin's Ear in the 1740s to convince Admiralty and Parliament of the need for a permanent Marine Corps. So useful did this Corps prove that in 1802 it received the distinction 'Royal', an honour borne by only the most distinguished

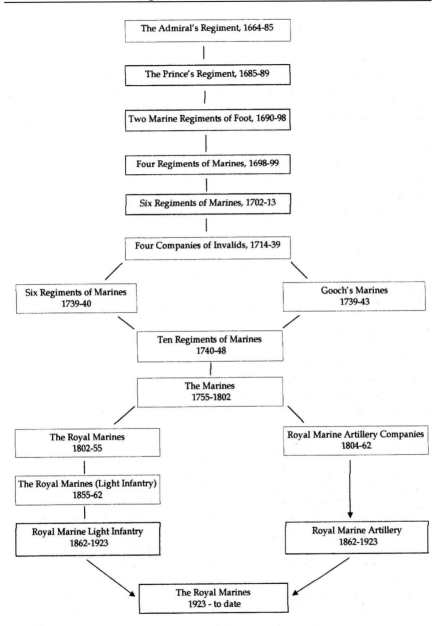

Figure 1: Evolution of the Royal Marines.

regiments. Earl St Vincent, then First Lord of the Admiralty, commented,

> I never knew an appeal made to them for honour, courage, or loyalty
> that they did not more than realize my highest expectations. If ever the
> hour of real danger should come to England they will be found the
> country's sheet anchor.

The Grand Divisions' longevity owed much to Victorian Britain's social
and strategic stability. The Corps was no longer a threat to freedom, more a
career opportunity for younger sons of the political classes. Economic difficulties following the First World War (1914–18) brought amalgamation of the
RMA and RMLI in 1923, but operational roles and administrative methods
altered little until the Second World War (1939–45). Since then economic
decline and loss of naval supremacy have demanded a leaner organization
and a move away from sea service. Today's Royal Marines are organized into
functional groups. Chatham Division and the Depot at Deal have gone. Royal
Marine Commandos, the fighting units, are based in the West Country and
Scotland. Only the band service remains at Portsmouth. The new organization is good value for the tax payer, but problematical for the family
historian.

1.2.1 Marine regiments

The ninety years before the marines became a unified corps saw a multiplicity
of marine regiments come and go. The distinction between a 'corps' and a
'regiment' is crucial. A 'corps' is a body of troops intended for some special
purpose, for example medical or engineering. Such formations answer to a
government department, such as the Board of Ordnance in the case of the
Royal Engineers (RE), and represent the sole accredited repository of expertise
in their field. A regiment, on the other hand, is one of several similar formations making up one branch of the army. Early British infantry regiments
consisted of six or more companies of 50–200 men each.

Most regiments during this period took their titles from their colonel, to
whom the Crown sub-contracted much of the administration now done by
government agencies. Colonels ran their units on credit, and profited finan-
cially from raising, clothing, paying and even arming their men, as did
captains of companies. A regiment was a source of patronage, through the
appointment of junior officers and the placement of contracts. Anyone
researching marine ancestors between 1689 and 1748 needs to know in which
regiments they may have served, as well as with which ships.

There were four incarnations of marine regiments between 1664 and 1748:

4

1. The Duke of York and Albany's Maritime Regiment of Foot was formed in accordance with an Order in Council of 28 October 1664, with six companies of 200 men. Regiments of the New Model Army had served at sea under Cromwell's Republic, but these were the first 'land Souldjers' raised specifically 'to be distributed into His Majesty's Fleets prepared for Sea Service'. Since James Duke of York was Lord High Admiral, the regiment is often known as the Admiral's Regiment. It changed name twice, first to the Duke's, when James ceased to be Lord High Admiral in 1673, then to Prince George of Denmark's Maritime Regiment, when James II became king in 1685. Also known as the Prince's Regiment, the unit maintained close links with its original colonel. Many of its men deserted after the Glorious Revolution of 1688, when James fled the country. The whole regiment was disbanded on 28 February 1689 as politically unreliable.

2. The 1st and 2nd Marine Regiments of Foot were raised for the Nine Years' War of 1689–97, which pitted England's new rulers, William III and Queen Mary, against Louis XIV of France. Commissions were issued on 16 January 1690, though recruiting was already under way. Each regiment had three battalions of 500, increasing the marine establishment to 3,000. The original colonels were the Earls of Torrington and Pembroke. The former was succeeded by the Marquis of Carmarthen, and the latter by Sir Henry Killegrew, Lord John Berkely, and Sir Cloudesley Shovell. At the end of the war the two regiments were merged with three army regiments, seeking to escape disbandment by rebadging as marines. Parliament saw through the ruse, and disbanded the lot on 20 May 1690. Any marines still at sea appeared on the ship's books as seamen.

3. Six regiments of marines were raised in 1702, following renewed hostilities with France. Officers were commissioned on 10 March. Colonels were:

   1st. Thomas Saunderson; T Pownall; Charles Wills.
   2nd. George Villiers; Alexander Luttrell; Joshua Churchill; Sir Harry Goring.
   3rd. Edward Fox; John Bor.
   4th. Henry Mordaunt (transferred to army 1703 and re-raised); William Seymour (transferred to army 1710 and re-raised); Charles Churchill.
   5th. Henry Holt.
   6th. Viscount Shannon.

These regiments must have been well over strength as the marine establishment rose to 8,000. Britain's withdrawal from the war in 1711 soon brought calls for their disbandment. Instructions were drawn up on 28 June 1713, commissioners paying the men off amidst scenes of considerable disorder. Churchill's, Holt's and Shannon's were disbanded, the other units transferring to the Irish establishment to escape parliamentary scrutiny (see section 1.6).

4. Ten regiments of marines were formed after the outbreak of the War of Jenkin's Ear against Spain. Six mustered in October 1739, and four more in December 1740. Including extra companies raised for sea service, the marine establishment numbered 10,000. Placed under the Army to prevent marine and naval officers colluding to defraud the Treasury, 1st to 10th Marines were numbered 44th to 53rd Foot respectively. They were also known by their colonel's name. The succession of colonels appears in Richard Brooks's *The Royal Marines* Appendix 2.

Three more regiments of 1,000 were raised in 1741 in New York, then a British colony. Thirty young gentlemen with military experience went out from home to serve as lieutenants, but most officers were members of American provincial assemblies or plantation owners. The men were Irish Roman Catholics, straight off the quayside. Reorganized under a Colonel Gooch as a single regiment of four battalions, they ranked as 43rd Foot.

Subordinating marines to the army was not a success. Corruption ran wild while marine detachments went in rags. The Duke of Cumberland complained they were 'neither sea nor land forces'. The Admiralty took over on 28 February 1747, but the war was nearly done. Recruiting stopped in June 1748, and all ten regiments disbanded by the end of the year.

These transient marine regiments were employed as might have been expected, except the Admiral's. Despite its title and mission statement, the regiment had no monopoly of sea service. Other regiments contributed to the fleet: over 1,000 Foot Guards and Coldstreamers went to sea in 1665. After the naval wars of the 1660s and 1672, the Admiral's became indistinguishable from other regiments of Charles II's army. It was dispersed around England as a gendarmerie, doing most of its fighting with Excise men, or amongst themselves. Early Corps historians claimed the Admiral's were quartered near the home ports, but records do not support this.

The first true marines were William and Mary's two regiments in the 1690s, kept at sea or in readiness for embarkation, sometimes working in naval dockyards. They suffered heavy losses in the Battle of Beachy Head (30 June 1690). Queen Anne's marine regiments fought throughout the War of the Spanish Succession (1701–11) as ship's detachments, for example at the decisive action of Malaga (13 August 1705). As amphibious landing forces they distinguished themselves at Gibraltar (1704–5), Barcelona (1705), Alicante (1706) and Minorca (1708).

The six regiments raised in 1739 had the misfortune to take part in one of the most disastrous amphibious campaigns ever undertaken by British forces. An attempt to capture Cartagena, now in Colombia, saw the largest commitment of marines to a single operation before the First World War. Nine-tenths of the troops died, having failed in all their objectives. Marine officer casualties exceeded the initial establishment: one general commanding, 21 field officers, 55 captains, and 130 subalterns. Wolfe's Marines had 96 men fit for duty out of 1,000. Nothing was left of some regiments but their name. Sent to the West Indies under the deluded impression that they could withstand the climate, Gooch's Marines did no better.

All marine regiments suffered from catastrophic neglect, except possibly the Admiral's, which never went to sea very much. Administrative arrangements barely acceptable ashore were disastrous for troops at sea. Regiments were paid only after being mustered as a whole. This was impossible for small detachments scattered around the fleet, even if those responsible had done their duty. As it was, officers of detachments omitted to submit lists of men under their command, ships' books failed to identify regiments and companies, ships' captains prevented marine officers checking their men were entered correctly and transferred men between ships without their officers' knowledge. A marine serving in the Mediterranean in 1746 was presumed dead after removing to another ship, 'till by Accident he was found in a return from Southampton'.

Clothing was issued annually on 11 June from regimental sources. It rarely reached detachments, while ships' pursers would not issue marines with 'slops', or sailor's working clothes. Admiral Russell reported in 1695, 'the Marine Soldiers of the 1st Marine Regiment are in a manner naked for want of Cloaths'. *Devonshire*'s marines petitioned the Admiralty in 1706, with her captain's support, complaining that, 'since the raising of the Regiment and our listing [in 1702] wee have recd but one whole mounting of clothes, being now almost naked for want'. Such inefficiency offended even eighteenth-century sensibilities, and contributed to the high wastage rates among marine regiments.

These early regiments leave an indistinct trail for the family historian, particularly for other ranks. Marine Pay Office records include 394 bundles of Effective and Subsistence Lists (ADM 96) for 1688 to 1837 (like other official Admiralty and War Office papers held at the National Archives or TNA, these are identified by a reference number beginning ADM or WO, in this case ADM 96). Ships' Muster Lists may include early marines, who were not at this time entered separately from the seamen. Two relevant series are ADM 36 and 37 for 1688 to 1858, and ADM 39 for 1667–1798. Officers are easier to trace, their commissions appearing in the *London Gazette*. However, this was not indexed at this early period. A Commissions and Appointments Register (ADM 6/405) survives in date order for 1703–13, as does a run of Royal Warrants for Commission 1664-1747 in *State Papers Domestic, Military Entry Books* (SP 44/164-188). *Calendars of State* and *Treasury Papers*, compiled and indexed in the nineteenth century, often mention individuals. Denunciations by marine officers of plots to burn down Sheerness dockyard mingle with reports of battles such as Sole Bay in 1672, the first occasion 'marines' are officially described as such. Petitions for financial or other relief provide rare insights into the lives of individuals.

1.2.2 The Grand Divisions
The continuous history of the Royal Marines dates from an Order in Council of 3 April 1755, establishing a single Corps of marines:

> to serve on board Your Majesty's ships and vessels at such times, in such proportions, and under such orders and regulations as Your High Admiral or Commissioners of the Admiralty shall judge proper.

Government recognized that marines were neither an inferior sort of infantry, who could be raised and disbanded at will, nor an *ersatz* seaman, but a distinct sort of fighting man sharing some attributes of both. An effective marine force requires a separate identity reflecting its special function, a coherent unified administration, and continuity of existence, allowing development of expertise and esprit de corps. The measures laid down in 1755 to put these principles into practice shaped marine organization for nearly two centuries.

The Order in Council abandoned the regimental model. The new marine establishment consisted of three 'Grand Divisions', with permanent headquarters at Chatham, Portsmouth and Plymouth. These were administrative organizations, having nothing in common with later combat formations such as the Royal Naval Division (RND) formed in 1914 or the RM Division of the Second World War. Concentration at the Royal Navy's home ports ensured a critical mass of marines fit for sea, ready for unforeseen emergencies. Marines rarely transferred between divisions, which played a central role in their lives. When a ship decommissioned, its marine detachment always returned to its own division. When John Howe, a Plymouth marine, left the *Serpent* at Sheerness in December 1793, he and his four comrades were allowed twenty-one days to walk back to headquarters.

Individual marines belonged to one of fifty numbered companies. Many accounts give the initial 1755 establishment as 5,000, which is not strictly correct as it omits NCOs. Each company consisted of 100 Private marines, with a proportion of sergeants, corporals and drummers, bringing total strength up

Church parade at Chatham in the 1920s, showing the eighteenth-century barracks, since demolished.

A TABLE of the Quarters of the Marine Companies, with the Numbers stationed at each.

Chatham.	Portsmouth.	Plymouth.
1st Comp.	2d Comp.	3d Comp.
4th	5th	6th
7th	8th	9th
10th	11th	12th
13th	14th	15th
16th	17th	18th
19th	20th	21st
22d	23d	24th
25th	26th	27th
28th	29th	30th
31st	32d	33d
34th	35th	36th
37th	38th	39th
40th	41st	42d
43d	44th	45th
46th	47th	48th
	49th	50th
	51st	52d
	53d	54th
	55th	56th
	57th	58th
	59th	60th
	61st	62d
	63d	64th
	65th	66th
	67th	68th
	69th	70th
16 Comp.	27 Comp.	27 Comp.

[1775]

A TABLE of the QUARTERS Of the ROYAL MARINE COMPANIES, With the Numbers stationed at each.

Chatham. Companies.		Portsmouth. Companies.		Plymouth. Companies.		Woolwich. Companies.	
1st	73d	2d	74th	3d	75th	144th	168th
4th	76th	5th	77th	6th	78th	145th	169th
7th	79th	8th	80th	9th	81st	146th	170th
10th	82d	11th	83d	12th	84th	147th	171st
13th	85th	14th	86th	15th	87th	148th	172d
16th	88th	17th	89th	18th	90th	149th	173d
19th	91st	20th	92d	21st	93d	150th	
22d	94th	23d	95th	24th	96th	151st	
25th	97th	26th	98th	27th	102d	152d	
28th	100th	29th	101st	30th	105th	153d	
31st	103d	32d	104th	33d	108th	154th	
34th	106th	35th	107th	36th	111th	155th	
37th	109th	38th	110th	39th	114th	156th	
40th	112th	41st	113th	42d	117th	157th	
43d	115th	44th	116th	45th	120th	158th	
46th	118th	47th	119th	48th	123d	159th	
49th	121st	50th	122d	51st	126th	160th	
52d	124th	53d	125th	54th	129th	161st	
55th	127th	56th	128th	57th	132d	162d	
58th	130th	59th	131st	60th	135th	163d	
61st	133d	62d	134th	63d	137th	164th	
64th		65th	136th	66th	139th	165th	
67th		68th	138th	69th	141st	166th	
70th		71st	140th	72d	143d	167th	
Art'y Comp' 1st		Art'y Comp' 2d	142d	Art'y Comp' 3d		Art'y Comp' 4th	
48 Comp'.		49 Comp'.		49 Comp'.		31 Comp'.	

[1805]

Head Quarters OF THE ROYAL MARINE (LIGHT INFANTRY AND ARTILLERY) COMPANIES.
(One hundred and thirty-three.)

Chatham. 1st Division.	Portsmouth. 2nd Division.	Plymouth. 3rd Division.	Woolwich. 4th Division.	Fort Cumberland. Artillery Division.
28 Companies.	30 Companies.	30 Companies.	28 Companies.	17 Companies.
1st	2nd	3rd	4th	1st
5th	6th	7th	8th	2nd
9th	10th	11th	12th	3rd
13th	14th	15th	16th	4th
17th	18th	19th	20th	5th
21st	22nd	23rd	24th	6th
25th	26th	27th	28th	7th
29th	30th	31st	32nd	8th
33rd	34th	35th	36th	9th
37th	38th	39th	40th	10th
41st	42nd	43rd	44th	11th
45th	46th	47th	48th	12th
49th	50th	51st	52nd	13th
53rd	54th	55th	56th	14th
57th	58th	59th	60th	15th
61st	62nd	63rd	64th	16th
65th	66th	67th	68th	17th
69th	70th	71st	72nd	
73rd	74th	75th	76th	
77th	78th	79th	80th	
81st	82nd	83rd	84th	
85th	86th	87th	88th	
89th	90th	91st	92nd	
93rd	94th	95th	96th	
97th	98th	99th	100th	
101st	102nd	103rd	104th	
105th	106th	109th	111th	
113th	107th	110th	112th	
	108th	115th	116th	
	114th			

[1859]

Tables of companies and their divisions for 1775, 1805 and 1859, showing the expansion of the Corps.

to 5,500 other ranks. There were also 50 captains, 150 subalterns, and nine senior officers: a lieutenant colonel, a major and an adjutant at each division.

As with the Grand Divisions, these divisional companies were administrative units, never mustered as a whole. Taken in conjunction with a man's division, his company number is the essential key to unlocking the relevant corps records. If a marine's company is known, it is possible to deduce his division, as companies belonged to particular divisions. The original numbering sequence began at Portsmouth with Company No.1, proceeding clockwise to Plymouth for No.2, and Chatham for No.3, and so on. The sequence varied over time, but at any given date a man's company number relates uniquely to his division, as shown in the illustration on page 10. Private John Brooks, who served in *Victory* in 1805, is shown by his officer's notebook at the Royal Marines Museum to have been in Company No.4. He was, therefore, a Chatham marine, following the 1763 reordering of the companies. This makes sense as *Victory* was a Chatham-based ship.

About a third of the Corps might be at divisional headquarters at one time. While there, the men formed a number of parade companies. These were quite distinct from the divisional companies described above, being used for drill and other domestic purposes. The new Corps had few field officers, that is, colonels and majors, compared with the regiments they replaced. This was a reasonable economy. Sir Charles Littleton of the Duke's Regiment had questioned sending even junior officers to sea, 'for no land officer above a corporal does or can signify anything a shipboard above the rate of a private soldier'. Field officers were exempted from sea service, their main responsibility being to run the three headquarters and the Marine Office in London. The Corps' first commanding officer was Colonel James Paterson, his instructions requiring him, 'to have a room near the Admiralty Office for the Dispatch of Business'. Besides Paterson three colonels commandant were accountable to the Admiralty for the efficiency of their division, with no intervening authority to impede the flow of orders and directives one way, and reports and requests the other.

Marines lived in ale-houses and other licensed premises, as British soldiers always had. The consequences for discipline and local people were unfortunate. Drunken marines wandered the streets, deserted, or fought civilians. Local magistrates retaliated with vexatious proceedings against members of the Corps. To prevent these nuisances, and achieve its aim of massing marines near their embarkation points, the Admiralty took the revolutionary step of housing them in barracks. A converted victualling store at Portsmouth was the first marine barracks to be occupied in April 1769, followed in September 1779 by a new building at Chatham, and by Stonehouse Barracks at Plymouth in 1783.

Victorian engraving of the parade ground at Stonehouse Barracks, Plymouth.

The Admiralty's investment in property and its flexible administrative arrangements achieved two aims. They provided the basis for rapid wartime expansion, either by adding men to existing companies or raising new ones. At the end of the American War of Independence in 1782 there were 25,000 marines in 151 companies. The year after Trafalgar there were over 30,000 marines in 183 companies, 30 belonging to a new division at Woolwich. The divisional system also managed peacetime retrenchment, without dissipating hard-won experience and esprit de corps. All four divisions survived the Napoleonic Wars, although reduced to just 6,000 marines in 102 companies by 1817.

The operational role of the new Corps of Marines resembled that of previous marines. Their most significant service numerically was as ships' detachments, fighting in the classic naval actions of the Seven Years' War (1757–63), the American War of Independence (1775–82), the French Revolutionary War (1793–1801), and the Napoleonic Wars (1802–15). Their more visible role, away from the Royal Navy's glory-hunters, was as independent battalions landed in support of military operations ashore. Some were formed from marines of the fleet, as in Egypt in 1801. Others came from the pool of marines at headquarters. Sometimes there were still too few marines. Whole regiments of conventional infantry were shipped as marines in the 1790s (see section 1.6). The award of the title 'Royal Marines' on 29 April 1802 coincides with the end of such makeshifts.

The advent of Grand Divisions is a defining moment for the researcher as well as the marine. The Admiralty's anxiety lest the Corps fall into the destructive ways of previous marine regiments led to creation of a mass of records: attestation papers; description, discharge and embarkation books; general weekly returns; letter and order books. Each division kept its own records, narrowing the field of research once that key piece of information is known. Organizational stability provides a remarkable degree of procedural consistency between the mid-eighteenth and mid-twentieth century. Unfortunately the survival of Royal Marine records is uneven. Despite the Admiralty's efforts, it is a matter of chance whether any particular document still exists.

1.2.3 Red and Blue Marines
Marines featured in paintings of Nelson's battles appear without exception in red, the traditional colour of the British infantry. Today, on special occasions, their successors wear blue. For a time individual marines wore both. The transformation is not just of interest to military tailors, as it illustrates the development of the Corps up to the 1920s.

The traditional role of marines in a sea action was to provide disciplined, accurate small arms fire, a more complex task than working great guns, which could be left to seamen. The Royal Navy's makeshift recruitment policies prevented the development of a pool of skilled seamen gunners, but in the eighteenth century that did not matter very much. Smooth-bore guns were simple enough to operate effectively at the close ranges favoured by sea captains. When the navy needed artillery expertise, as they did to deliver high angle fire from the heavy mortars carried in bomb vessels, they called on the Royal Artillery.

The obsession of naval officers with summary corporal punishment, which was illegal in the army, caused friction whenever soldiers had to serve at sea. Most of the infantrymen embarked in the 1790s were put ashore after successful military appeals against naval courts martial. The only soldiers left on board HM ships were the unfortunate artillerymen in bomb vessels. When artillery officers supported their men's refusal to do more than serve their mortars, the Admiralty decided to raise its own corps of artillery. These were

Royal Marine artillerymen outside the Main Gate at Eastney in the early 1900s. Similar scenes would have been seen outside every barracks.

inevitably marines, being the navy's only permanently embodied men, with a shore establishment to train in.

An Order in Council of 18 August 1804 established a company of Royal Marine Artillery at each headquarters, selected from the most intelligent and experienced officers and men of their divisions. At first indistinguishable from other marines, the new artillerymen adopted dark blue coats by 1814, a more practical colour for working with black powder. They became known as 'Blue Marines'. Other companies still wore red, hence 'Red Marines'.

Almost by accident the Admiralty had created the Royal Navy's first gunnery specialists, the RMA rapidly moving onto conventional naval and field guns. When the Admiralty established a gunnery school in HMS *Excellent* in 1831, it appointed a Lieutenant RMA with five NCOs and gunners to superintend the seamen under training. Defence cuts temporarily reduced the RMA to just two companies, but the growing complexity of naval weapons brought their numbers to 3,000 by the end of the 1850s. RMA personnel were then concentrated at Fort Cumberland, east of Portsmouth. They became an administratively independent division in 1862, moving to their new headquarters at Eastney between 1864 and 1867.

Red Marines still provided most ships' detachments and battalions for shore operations, accompanied by RMA field batteries. Portsmouth Division outgrew Clarence Barracks in Pembroke Road, moving to Forton Barracks in Gosport in 1848. Establishment of a single Depot at Deal or Walmer in May 1861 was a rare example of divisional integration. All marine recruits received initial training there before going on to their permanent division. Gunners were not recruited directly, the RMA taking its pick from other divisions. Following the Crimean War Red Marines acquired the honorific status of light infantry, becoming known in 1862 as Royal Marine Light Infantry (RMLI), an entirely separate entity from the RMA. Woolwich Division, known as the 'Court Division' from its proximity to London, was disbanded in 1869.

Meanwhile social and technological changes were calling the whole basis of both Corps into question. The 1853 Continuous Service Act resolved the naval manning problems that inspired the eighteenth-century experiments with marines. Seamen now remained in service between commissions, no longer temperamental birds of passage but picked men, with no need for marines to discipline them. Steam engines altered the whole system of naval warfare. As steam power replaced 'handraulics', work parties of big marines became unnecessary. Within fifty years of the Crimean War Sir John Colomb could speak of 'mastless ships resembling great floating fortresses, and entirely worked by labour saving machinery'. Rifled cannon outranged small arms men, and Gatling guns threatened to sweep them off the deck, threatening the marine's ability to fulfil his primary combat role.

The Royal Navy was slow to change. Older naval officers, grown up before continuous service, found their marine detachments comforting. Veterans of naval brigades refused to believe sailors could replace marines ashore. However anomalous the Corps might look, it remained a popular force, more easily recruited than the Guards, fulfilling its historical function of supplementing the manpower of the navy. Far seeing marine officers argued that the reduced need for seamanship in a steam navy made it easier to augment sailors with marines, who should all be gunners. Naval expansion in the 1890s made it impossible to man all the guns of a growing fleet with sailors and RMA. Only first class battleships carried RMA detachments from 1892, their place in smaller ships taken by RMLI. By the First World War it was customary for marines to man a main armament turret, and a group of secondary guns in all battleships and cruisers. Gunnery qualifications were so widespread that 'trained in gunnery' was discontinued as a rate. All marines were expected to reach that standard.

The Grand Divisions still resembled those of the eighteenth century, with larger staffs to handle the administrative requirements of a modern corps. The Royal Marines' senior executive officer in 1914 was the adjutant general, successor to the old marine colonel commandants in town. Like them he was attached to the Admiralty, conveying its orders to the divisions. Each division, including the Deal depot, had a colonel commandant, assisted by another full colonel responsible for pay and clothing, and the accounts of the quartermasters, now three in number. A number of lieutenant colonels supervised the divisional 'battalion', inspected men embarking or returning from sea service, and instructed junior officers and men in their military duties. Majors were no longer exempt from sea service, every flagship having a major of marines to command the squadron's combined detachments when landed as a battalion. At headquarters they acted as gunnery and musketry instructors, or as drafting officer responsible for the sea service rosters of men ready for embarkation. Captains and subalterns commanded the eight battalion companies, the demand for captains to command ships' detachments giving many lieutenants their own company. The adjutant was a crucial figure, answering directly to the colonel commandant for divisional standards of drill, instruction, dress and behaviour.

When the First World War began there were 3,393 Blue and 13,425 Red Marines, rising to 7,640 and 24,444 by the Armistice. Many were short service 'Hostilities Only' or 'HO' marines, enlisted for the war's duration, a new departure for the Corps. About half of all First World War Royal Marines served at sea. Such was the country's financial plight afterwards the Treasury sought to disband the Corps entirely, as in 1713 and 1748. In the event the Corps was reduced to 9,500 by amalgamating Portsmouth's RMLI division with the RMA at Eastney in 1923. RMA officers grumbled that amalgamation was a euphemism for abolition, but the move had merits. The two types of marine had been functionally indistinguishable for years. The change restored the Corps' single identity and clarified its function, making it easier to defend against further cuts. The sartorial consequence of amalgamation was replacement of red by the dark blue uniform worn as full dress today.

Victorian marines, unlike their predecessors, rarely saw action at sea. The destruction of the French and Spanish fleets at Trafalgar began a period of British naval supremacy unchallenged until the 1890s. Most of the Royal Navy's active service in the nineteenth century was ashore, in which Royal Marines played their full part (see section 3.1.2). The divisional system's ability to mobilize extra battalions resulted in Battalions RM participating in numerous campaigns independently of the navy (section 3.2.1). The First World War saw the Royal Navy's first fleet action for over a century at Jutland (31 May 1916). Ashore, however, Royal Marines were as ubiquitous as the army's plum and apple jam, serving from Antwerp to Zeebrugge, most significantly with the RND at Gallipoli and on the Western Front (sections 3.2.2 & 3.2.3).

Royal Marine administration remained essentially unaltered. Major changes were separation of the RMA in 1859–62, Woolwich Division's transient existence, and creation of the Depot at Deal. For the first fifty-eight years of their existence the records of Royal Marine artillerymen, ranking as gunners or bombardiers, should be sought with those of their parent division. Ships' muster lists disappear towards the end of the century, though from the 1850s onwards individual parchment service records provide a gold mine of information for those lucky enough to have inherited them. At the same time increasing literacy and economic prosperity brought both more and new records. Marine officers had always kept diaries and written letters. Nineteenth-century other ranks did so too. They also opened accounts with banks and building societies. Records of the Corps' own Savings Bank are at the National Archives.

1.2.4 The green beret

The Royal Marines have seen more fundamental change since the 1920s than in the preceding century and a half. From being a naval white elephant, unsure of its future and threatened with disbandment, the Corps has become the linchpin of the Royal Navy's power projection capability.

The interwar years were slack water for the armed forces in general. Little coherent attempt was made to refashion them to suit Britain's constrained financial situation, or to reflect the lessons of the First World War. Official instructions restated the Corps' function of providing detachments, 'fully capable of manning their share of the gun armament of ships, [and] specially trained to provide a striking force, drawn either from the Divisions or from the Fleet'. Just how ships might operate with a third of their gun crews ashore, or how marines on extended cruises might maintain the skills required by modern land warfare, was not explained.

When the Second World War broke out in September 1939, Royal Marine numbers had reached 12,390. The regular Corps, however, was fully committed at sea and could not be spared for operations ashore. HO marines were recruited to form a striking force consisting of the RM Division and the Mobile Naval Base Defence Organizations (MNBDO I and II). None of these justified the effort expended upon them. When British strategists thought about offensive operations after the fall of France, they turned to the army.

The raiding directive of 17 June 1940 created a Combined Operations Organization (COO), 'to harass the enemy and cause him to disperse his forces, and to create material damage'. Its commander was Lieutenant General A G B Bourne RM, but the first raiding companies consisted of Army volunteers. Christened 'commandos' after the Boer guerrilla fighters of the South African War (1899–1902), their personnel received green berets on passing the rigorous training course. Thus the green beret associated with today's Royal Marines was first worn by soldiers. Depending on context, 'commando' may mean either a small body of shock troops, or an individual member of such a unit. A few individual marines volunteered, but amphibious raiding was not seen as a task for the Corps in general. Somehow the independent companies acquired the title of 'Special Service' units, only shedding the initials 'SS', with their unwelcome connotations of Hitler's infamous *Schutzstaffel* in November 1944. By then Britain's fortunes and those of the Royal Marines had improved beyond recognition.

The tide turned when America joined the war in December 1941, opening the way for an assault upon Hitler's Europe. The commandos were reorganized and expanded, using manpower from the RM Division and MNBDOs. Formed at Deal in February 1942, 'The RM Commando' had already participated in the disastrous Dieppe raid on 19 August 1942. A second RM Commando was raised in October, the two units known as 'A' and 'B' before renumbering as 40 and 41. Organization reflected their light raiding role: a small headquarters with four troops of 100 lettered A, B, X and Y, a reminder of the Royal Navy's system of identifying gun turrets.

The big change came in 1943, when the RM Division and MNBDOs were dissolved to create another six RM Commandos. Most, however, became landing craft crew, resuming the Corps' ancient function of supplementing naval manpower. The following November a Special Service Group of four brigades brought together all eight Army and eight RM Commandos (later nine) under General Robert Sturges, the RM Division's erstwhile commander. Half in jest, a senior officer parodied Earl St Vincent's dying words: 'If ever the hour of real danger comes to England the Royal Marines will be found busy reorganizing themselves.' This revolution from above gave the Royal Marines a new but entirely appropriate job, and saved them from extinction. By the end of hostilities Corps' numbers had reached 78,500, reflecting the multitude of roles it was playing. Total casualties for all ranks between 1939 and 1945 numbered 3,999 dead and 3,543 wounded, an unusual disproportion, reflecting the heavy loss of life at sea.

Army Commandos fell immediate victims to postwar defence cuts. Three RM Commandos survived within a reduced Corps of 13,000, headed now by a Commandant General RM (CGRM). Individual units were renumbered to commemorate theatres in which they had fought: 40 Commando for the Mediterranean, 42 for the Far East and 45 for north-west Europe. A less cosmetic change was the end of the divisional system in 1947, when the Corps reorganized along functional instead of geographic lines. Chatham took responsibility for pay, records, drafting and NCOs' promotion, Portsmouth for sea service training, and Plymouth for infantry skills. The end of nearly 200 years of divisional administration was underlined by closure of Chatham Group in 1950. Numbers fell to 10,300, but total disbandment was avoided.

The new structure suited the uncertain postwar strategic environment: the withdrawal from empire that ended at Aden in 1967; the defensive stands against the Soviet Union and IRA, and the armed interventions that followed the end of the Cold War in 1989. An administratively leaner Corps proved large enough to support creation and reduction of additional units, such as 41 Independent Commando of 1950–2, without losing vital skills and traditions. During the 1960s 41 and 43 Commandos reformed and disbanded as required, rather like the old Battalions RM. More recently, Fleet Protection Group RM (FPGRM) evolved from Comacchio Company, tasked with protecting the Royal Navy's nuclear submarines at Faslane in Scotland, and general ship security, for example on the Armilla Patrol in the Persian Gulf.

Today (2007) 3 Commando Brigade includes three Commandos RM. It is supported by a Royal Artillery Regiment and Royal Engineers Squadron, both commando-trained and wearing the green beret, besides the Commando Logistic Regiment, a mixture of Royal Marines, army supply and ordnance specialists, and RN medical staff. Despite competition from nuclear weapons, naval aviation and surface warships, the Royal Navy has renewed its fleet of specialist landing ships twice since the Second World War. Royal Marines continue to man the landing craft carried by these larger ships. Together these vessels allow the Royal Marines to act as the nucleus of the amphibious forces of the Crown, as they did with startling effect in the Falkland Islands in 1982.

Royal Marines fought in all the Royal Navy's big gun actions of the Second World War. Ashore they shared in the war's early disasters in Norway (April–May 1940), Crete (May–June 1941), and Singapore (February 1942). When the tide turned they led the Allied return to Europe in Sicily and Italy (July and September 1943). The invasion of Normandy on D-Day (6 June 1944) saw the largest ever single commitment of Royal Marines: five out of eight commandos present, reinforced ships' detachments, landing craft crew, an armoured support group of Centaur tanks, plus MNBDO provost, signals, beach control and port clearing parties. Since 1945 Royal Marines have fought in every conceivable environment: the jungles of Malaysia during the Malayan Emergency (1949–52) and confrontation with Indonesia (1962–4), the deserts of South Arabia (1960–7), the streets of Northern Ireland, the marshes of southern Iraq, and the mountains of Korea and Afghanistan. Almost the only thing unchanged since permanent establishment of the Corps in 1755 is the worldwide scope of its operations.

The end of the Grand Divisions has complicated the task of the family historian. Until the late 1940s individual service records were held at division. In 1947 personnel administration transferred to a centralized Pay and Records Office RM (PRORM), later the Drafting and Records Office RM (DRORM): see Chapter 4 for contact details current at publication. Records for marines serving since 1928, however, are available only to next of kin.

1.3 MARENS (the RM answer to Wrens)

The first women to serve officially in the Royal Navy belonged to the Women's Royal Naval Service (WRNS or Wrens), during the First World War. Facing a desperate shortage of manpower in 1917 the Admiralty recruited women, under female officers, for shore-based duties as cooks, mess stewards, clerks, telephonists, storekeepers and more daringly as motor-cycle despatch riders, boat crews and fitters. By the end of 1918 WRNS numbers exceeded 7,000, some of whom served at Royal Marine establishments.

The WRNS demobilized in 1919, reforming on 21 February 1939 with the renewed threat of war. By 1944 there were over 74,000 Wrens, supplementing their previous activities with more technical roles as armourers, mechanics and meteorologists. When serving with Royal Marine units Wrens became known as Marens, the usual tally band on the hat being replaced by a red patch set behind a Globe and Laurel cap badge.

Marens continued working with Royal Marine units, deploying to Northern Ireland with Commandos RM from 1978, and to Cyprus in 1979, until the WRNS absorbed into the Royal Navy in 1993. Women today do not serve as Royal Marines, except in the RM Band Service (see below). As Marens were naval personnel, their records are held with other WRNS records, as part of the Royal Navy's archives. Researchers should consult the guidebooks on tracing naval ancestry listed under Further Reading.

1.4 The Royal Marine Band Service and Royal Naval School of Music

Marines have always had musicians. Their history is complex, especially since the Royal Marines took responsibility for meeting the Royal Navy's musical requirements in 1903, as well as their own. Today's band service descends from three very different classes of musicians. Since 1979 they have formed part of a single organization. In the past they were members of very distinct establishments, performing different functions under different terms of service, and rarely transferring from one branch to another. The family historian needs to be aware of these distinctions, if only to avoid wasting time looking in wrong places.

1.4.1 The Corps of Drums

The first marine musicians were six drummers of the Duke's Regiment. Drummers were an essential part of their regiment. Marching in step to the beat of drum was a recent military innovation in the 1660s. Regiments beat up for recruits and beat retreat to end the day. On going into action they beat to arms, while ships beat to quarters. Bad hats might be drummed out of the service. In lighter moments drummers played on the fife, originally being known as whistlers, or *wifflers* in contemporary typography. Drummers always accompanied white flags to parley with the enemy, a diplomatic function justifying their status as junior NCOs. Any warship larger than a sloop included at least one drummer in their marine detachment. A 100-gun ship like the *Victory* carried three. Earl St Vincent made them an essential part of the ceremonial with which he bolstered naval discipline following the mutinies of the 1790s.

Bugles were introduced into the Royal Marines during the 1810s, replacing the drum for signalling purposes in the field and on board ship. 'Boy bugler' became an accepted route into the Corps for lads too young for private marines. As with drummers, ships' detachments included one or more buglers depending on the size

Royal Marines Band shoulder title: these brass letters worn on the tunic will identify a musician in the absence of headdress or instruments.

21

of the ship. HMS *Nelson*, the Royal Navy's largest battleship in 1939, carried three; HMS *Hood* and aircraft carriers had two; small cruisers one. Drummers and buglers were always an integral part of the Corps, despite marching at the head of every Royal Marine Band. They only became part of the band service in 1979.

1.4.2 Divisional bands

Portsmouth was probably the first Grand Division to acquire a band (in 1765), followed by Plymouth in 1767. Both employed six musicians, paid 6*d* extra a day, the Plymouth band directed by a civilian named Antonio Rocca. The bandsmen's duties were to attend daily at guard mounting, and march before the battalion to church on Sundays. Many had been professional musicians before enlisting, and they were much in demand. A Chatham divisional order insisted the band were not 'to be looked upon in the light of common fiddlers, and permitted at the desire of indifferent persons to play in that capacity at ordinary and common Balls and Concerts'. Portsmouth's band was thirty strong by the early nineteenth century, with clarinets, trombones, trumpets, flutes, oboes, bassoons and serpents.

Divisional bandsmen had no obligation to go to sea. This, combined with their fixed residence and opportunities to undertake paid engagements in their spare time, made their situation most attractive. The exception to their exclusion from active service was the First World War when divisional bands served six month tours in France with the RND. The RMA band also provided twenty musicians and four buglers for the Royal Yacht. The Portsmouth band continued this role until *Britannia* was decommissioned in 1997.

On the eve of the First World War there were five Royal Marine bands, one per division and one for the Depot at Deal. Five became four on amalgamation of the RMA and RMLI in 1923 and three in 1930, the Depot band disbanding when the Royal Naval School of Music moved to Deal (see below). Divisional bands could not escape the turmoil that followed the Second World War. Renamed Royal Marine Group Bands in 1947 they amalgamated with the Royal Naval School of Music in 1950 to create a single organization responsible for supplying bands for both Royal Navy and Royal Marines (see section 1.4.4). Buglers remained outside the new structure, although training had already transferred to the Royal Naval School of Music.

1.4.3 The Royal Naval School of Music

Naval vessels had bands from an early date. They do not require detailed description here, as they were not marines. Including numerous foreigners, they had little training beyond their musical qualifications, and little sympathy with naval traditions and discipline. As the Royal Navy became increasingly professional during the nineteenth century, this was no longer acceptable.

The Royal Marines' involvement in ships' bands began in 1874 when RM bandmasters were ordered to inspect the bands of training ships, and to issue certificates of competence. The Corps assumed general responsibility for naval music with an Order in Council of 20 May 1903 establishing a Royal Naval School of Music at Eastney. As ships returned from a commission their musicians were asked to transfer from the Royal Navy to the marines, future band ratings enlisting as Royal Marines. The new 'Royal Marine Bands' provided for all the Royal Navy's musical requirements, whether in naval establishments ashore or in ships anywhere in the world. Sometimes known as 'Navy Bands', they were entirely separate from the existing divi-

Royal Naval Band Service cap badge. Naval musicians were all Royal Marines from 1903, becoming the Royal Marines Band Service in 1950.

sional bands. The only way to transfer to one of the latter was to be discharged, and then audition. Previously naval bandsmen had been nobody's children while at sea. Now they were subject to the officer commanding the ship's RM detachment (OCRM), with generally beneficial effects.

When the First World War began the Royal Naval School of Music had an establishment of 1,450, providing fifty bands of between ten and two dozen musicians. Ceremonial duties at sea included 'Colours', when the white ensign was hoisted every morning, 'Divisions' every Sunday, and other more or less formal occasions. These might require playing as an orchestra, dance band, or jazz combo, as well as a conventional military band. RM bandsmen also played informally with other members of the crew, interwar photographs showing an improbable line-up of instruments.

The Royal Naval School of Music moved to Deal in October 1930, when it numbered just over a thousand. Peak strength was nearly 2,000 in the Second World War, including HO bandsmen and pensioners. There were eighty-four bands, fifty of them at sea. In 1950, however, the need for economy brought amalgamation with the surviving Group bands.

1.4.4 A single band service

A single Royal Marine Band Service was created on 1 September 1950 by amalgamating the Royal Naval School of Music with the Portsmouth and Plymouth Group bands. Chatham had disbanded in August. Royal Marine bandsmen lost their distinctive lyre collar badges, while the Group bands lost their immunity from being drafted. The service returned to Deal, after a confusing series of wartime moves away from the dangers of the south coast.

The new organization was 1,150 strong with thirty-six bands, including twenty-one at sea. This traditional role diminished rapidly during the 1950s, as large ships disappeared from the inventory. Total strength, all ranks, had fallen to 540 by 1 April 1973. The last warship to include an RM band as part of its complement was the aircraft carrier HMS *Ark Royal*, decommissioned in 1978.

Today (2007) there are five full strength Royal Marine bands, serving four RN and one RM establishment: in Portsmouth, Plymouth, Scotland, at *Britannia* Royal Naval College Dartmouth, and the Commando Training Centre Lympstone. The School of Music is now at Portsmouth, where it moved from Deal in 1996. Besides official tasks as military bands, orchestras and dance bands, their duties still bring them into the public eye, as they did in the eighteenth century. Royal Marine bandsmen are now trained to act as medical orderlies in wartime, which they did in the Falklands War and in the Gulf. Women first joined the band service in 1992, the only part of the Corps to recruit them. Since 1979 buglers have been part of the service, while preserving their own badges and career structure.

Records specifically devoted to the different band services are patchy. Buglers and members of divisional bands should appear with other members of their particular divisions. Buglers and Royal Marine bandsmen, when embarked, should appear in ships' records in the same way as other sea service marines. Royal Marine bandsmen may also appear in records kept by RMA clerks between 1903 and 1921, when the Royal Naval School of Music became administratively self-sufficient. Complications unique to the band service are:

1. The presence of both civilian and NCO instructors.
2. Changes in title from band colour sergeant and band sergeant before 1921 to bandmaster 1st or 2nd class, replaced in 1947 by bandmaster and band sergeant respectively.
3. The existence of both commissioned and warrant bandmasters.
4. The replacement of the term 'boy' in 1956 by 'junior musician'.

Against these problems, the badges worn by bandsmen are quite distinctive, for example their 'RMB' shoulder title. Musicians are highly photogenic, and

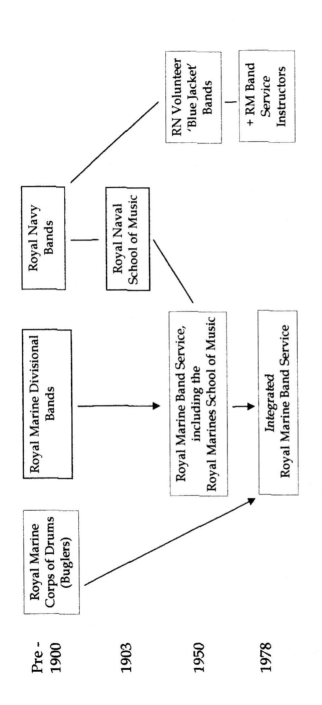

Figure 2: Evolution of the RM Band Service.

often took part in well publicized events, which may have left programmes or inspired news stories. Material evidence for a musical ancestor's life should, therefore, be relatively easier to find.

1.5 Ad hoc formations and detachments

The Royal Marines' capacity for expansion has attracted many functions, some with little obvious connection to the central purposes of the Corps. Most of the formations listed below existed only during the First World War. They are interesting to the family historian as they outnumbered the more glamorous combat units, fewer of whom can have survived to have children. The men were on short service engagements, and had little previous connection with the Royal Marines. Their records in most cases will be with the divisions to which they are shown as being affiliated.

1.5.1 Royal Marine units of the RND

The Royal Naval Division was formed in September 1914 without any of the engineers, transport and field ambulances that infantry divisions need to operate as a combat formation. These supporting services were manned through the Corps. Officers were a mixture of Royal Marines and specialists, such as Royal Engineers. Other ranks were usually civilians enrolled as Royal Marines, and affiliated to Deal for pay and records. Unit depots were at Blandford Camp with the RND depot. In the field the supporting services were inseparably bound up with the RND's fighting units. Throughout this section 'divisional' means belonging to the RND. It has nothing to do with RM Divisions at Chatham, etc.

a) Divisional engineers

The first supporting units raised were the divisional signal company and two (later three) field companies. A standard RE field company in 1914 numbered 6 officers, 211 men and 70 horses; a signal company 5 officers, 157 men, and 80 horses. There was no wireless communication within an infantry division. Messages were transmitted by cable, motor-cycle, or visual signal.

The first divisional engineers enrolled in the Royal Naval Volunteer Reserve (RNVR) and dressed as seamen, but also attested as Royal Marines. The Corps took over their administration in October 1914, the men enlisting henceforth as Royal Marines, whose uniform they wore with the Globe and Laurel badge. They were subject to the usual Corps conditions, but paid as RE. All four companies served with the RND at Gallipoli in 1915, returning with it to France in 1916.

When the RND was restyled 63rd (Royal Naval) Division the engineer companies became 63rd Divisional Signal Company, and 247, 248, and 249 Field Companies. In March 1917 the War Office had the divisional engineers transfer to the Royal Engineers. Personnel remained unchanged, though their records would no longer appear as Royal Marines. Casualties at that date numbered 56 killed or died and 158 wounded.

b) Divisional Train – Royal Marines
Military transport in 1914 was largely horse- or mule-drawn, presenting a maritime Corps with an unusual problem. Nevertheless, four companies and a headquarters were ready by January 1915, with the following establishment:

- Transport: 30 officers, 673 other ranks, 378 animals, 142 carts and wagons
- Medical: 1 officer, 175 other ranks, 16 animals, 21 motor ambulances

The men were RMLI reservists or RNVR volunteers. Affiliated to Deal, they were nominally on the books of HMS *Victory*, pay and accounts being dealt with at the RND offices. They were paid the same rates as the Army Service Corps (ASC), often holding such unusual ranks for marines as wheelers or farriers.

The train accompanied the division overseas, but did not generally land at Gallipoli, where the ground was unsuitable for wheeled transport. It spent most of 1915 in Egypt or Salonika. On rejoining the RND the unit was renumbered 63rd Divisional Train. Its idiosyncratic accounting arrangements allowed the train to escape transfer to the Army, serving as Royal Marines until after the Armistice in 1918. Casualties amounted to 27 killed or died, and 29 wounded.

c) Medical Unit – Royal Marines
The RND's original medical support was limited to battalion medical officers, a few naval sick berth attendants (SBAs) and Royal Marine Infirmary staff. Three divisional field ambulances were formed in November 1914. Officers were mostly temporary surgeons RN. Enlisted as Royal Marines, the men were affiliated to Deal for pay and records, but paid the same rates as the Royal Army Medical Corps (RAMC). Trained personnel were recruited through the St John's Ambulance Association. Many were coal miners from the north-east, their strong physique suiting them to the difficult task of carrying wounded men over broken terrain.

Each field ambulance consisted of nine medical officers, a lieutenant, quartermaster, sergeant-major and 171 other ranks. Most of the men were in four-man stretcher parties. The Medical Unit went ashore at Anzac and Helles, sharing the hard fighting of the Gallipoli campaign. The field ambulances

Men of the RM Medical Unit (note the Red Cross armbands) at Blandford Camp in 1916, before joining the RND in France.

renumbered 148, 149 and 150 on going to France. RAMC doctors replaced naval surgeons, but the men resisted attempts to take away their status as Royal Marines. Ordered to wear Red Cross arm bands in 1918, they bought red circled naval badges with their own money, rather than wear the RAMC issue. Casualties exceeded establishment, reflecting the risks of the service: 114 killed or died, and 555 wounded. Awards for gallantry were in proportion, with 128 Military Medals and 6 bars.

d) RM Motor Transport Company
Conscious of the RND's lack of mobility, the Admiralty purchased ninety model 'B' buses from the London General Omnibus Company in September 1914. The drivers were simultaneously attested as Royal Marines. They then drove down to Dover, before proceeding to Dunkirk. A number of gentlemen also volunteered to drive their own motor cars for £1 a day and reimbursement for the cost of tyres and petrol. This unlikely mixture of vehicles participated in the expedition to Antwerp, playing a vital role in evacuating stores and wounded.

The surviving buses with about seventy lorries were then attached to Army headquarters at St Omer, driving troops around the Ypres salient, often by night and under shell fire. The drivers remained on the Home Base Ledger at Eastney, with RMA numbers, their officers receiving RM commissions. Drivers were paid ten shillings a day compared with the ASC's six, but were said to be worth it. They saw service in First and Second Ypres, and during the Battles of Aubers Ridge and Festubert. The unit was incorporated into the ASC in August 1915. Few drivers would transfer into the army for less money, but some became drivers in the RMA Howitzer Brigade (see section 3.2.3).

1.5.2 Royal Marine Submarine Miners (RMSM)

The threat of U-boat attack inspired proposals in late 1914 to lay mine fields off estuaries too wide to protect with boom defences. There had been similar observation mines before the war, detonated from the shore, but they had been discontinued. A retired naval officer oversaw deployment of the mines as Captain of Defensive Mining, and a small force of Royal Marines was raised to watch and fire them, under naval control.

The nucleus of the RMSM was the Tyne Electrical Engineers, a Territorial Army unit with experience of submarine mining. These men transferred into the Royal Marines on 5 February 1915, being paid as RE with extra submarine mining pay. Officers received temporary commissions in the Corps. Many were local yachtsmen with knowledge of coastal waters, or qualified electrical engineers.

The RMSM was affiliated to Chatham Division, receiving Chatham register numbers, although headquarters was at Newcastle-on-Tyne until 1917. The depot was in Tynemouth Barracks, with detachments at Cromarty and Scapa Flow, where the Grand Fleet was stationed, and an experimental station at Felixstowe. As the war progressed the RMSM received drafts of invalids from the fighting fronts, expanding considerably under direction of the Admiral of Controlled Minefields. Late in 1918 its work merged with the anti-submarine activities of the 5th RM Battalion at Dover, but the unit remained distinct until it was demobilized.

1.5.3 Royal Marine Labour Corps (RMLC)

The RMLC had two components. The larger was stationed in French ports to handle stores for the British Expeditionary Force (BEF); the smaller was home service only.

a) France

Prompt unloading of the mass of supplies required by the BEF presented considerable difficulties for Naval Transport Officers (NTOs) at the base ports in France. NTOs needed a labour force under their direct control, but the personnel also had to be under local military discipline. The Royal Marine

Royal Marine Labour Corps cap badge (1917–18): serving in Britain and France during the First World War, usually in port or dock areas, this unit's members may be identified by this unique badge.

system of organization seemed to meet these contradictory requirements.

Two ASC companies of stevedores transferred to the Royal Marines on 2 February 1917 as a nucleus, supplemented by men who were over 41 (the age limit for combatant enlistment), but who wanted to do their bit. Officers were chosen from men with merchant navy or dockside experience. Many were promoted from the ranks. Administration was based partly at Chatham and partly at Deal, creating two separate series of attestation papers. Pay and records were located at Deal, the men being paid at ASC rates. To distinguish them from other troops they wore Royal Marine dark blue, without the red trouser stripe. Collar and cap badges were the Globe and Laurel, surmounted by a ship under sail.

Total RMLC strength was 57 officers and 4,853 other ranks, with a small number of RMLI to assist with discipline and administration. The Corps was distributed between Le Havre, Rouen, Trouville, Boulogne, Calais, Dunkirk, St Valery, Dieppe and Cherbourg, sometimes coming under aerial bombardment. Few of their 134 fatal casualties arose from enemy action, however. Some were accidental, but most were from disease, reflecting the advanced age of the men.

b) Home Service

No.1 (Home Service) Labour Company of the Royal Marines was raised to assist naval working parties handle the great number of mines required for North Sea mine-laying operations. Unit strength was 230 other ranks (Labour), with two RMLI officers and a handful of senior NCOs. Men were over-age, or from lower medical categories. They were paid ASC rates and affiliated to Chatham Division. The unit was stationed at Granton Mining Depot from 16 December 1917, and demobilized in 1919.

1.5.4 Royal Marine Engineers (RME)

Royal Marine Engineers served in both world wars, carrying out civil engineering tasks under military discipline. They should not be confused with combat units like the RND's Divisional Engineers.

a) First World War

The Admiralty formed the original RME to resolve the labour shortage of 1917, which was delaying urgent work at Scapa Flow. The unit followed the RMLC model, Royal Marines being responsible for discipline and administration, while technically qualified officers with temporary commissions directed the work. Many of the RMLI officers were Reserve warrant officers or NCOs given wartime commissions.

Divisional headquarters was at Chatham, with a small depot company to receive and equip recruits. Most of the personnel were in ten works companies, each 572 strong including a dozen RMLI and a mixture of craftsmen and unskilled pioneers. Recruits came from the Royal Engineers and lower medical categories, plus some conscientious objectors, all being paid at RE rates. By the Armistice numbers had risen to 10,000.

The RME's two main headquarters were in hutted camps at Southwick near Brighton and Bedmenham between Fareham and Gosport. Projects included an airfield at Scapa Flow and an oil pipeline between the Clyde and Forth. The unit demobilized soon after the Armistice, though small parties helped clear Ostend harbour and dismantle German fortifications on Heligoland.

b) Second World War

An Order in Council revived the RME on 19 March 1940. Headquarters was at Portsmouth with two 500-man companies camped at Freshwater on the Isle of Wight. By 1 August 1945 their establishment had risen to 257 officers and 7,764 men in battalions of 1,500 commanded by Lieutenant Colonels RM. As in the First World War the men consisted of skilled tradesmen and unskilled pioneers, paid as RE. A major change from the previous conflict was the use of heavy equipment such as bulldozers.

Second generation RMEs served around the world, repairing air raid damage, building airfields, camps and landing craft slipways, restoring captured ports, or installing refrigerators and fuel tanks. They came under fire at Anzio and Arromanches, once guarding an Italian caustic soda factory under shell fire. The RME disbanded in summer 1946, tradesmen having priority for demobilization.

1.5.5 Royal Marine Police (RMP)

Royal Marines have guarded dockyards intermittently since the 1690s, but during the nineteenth century the Metropolitan Police became responsible for policing dockyards and other naval facilities. The need for economy after the First World War persuaded the Admiralty to employ its own men.

An Order in Council of 13 October 1922 created a Royal Marine Police administered by the Adjutant General RM, and headed by its own chief constable from 1932. Officers were serving or retired RM or RN officers. Sergeants and constables were long service RM or RN pensioners, under 45, 'of such character and ability as to ensure that they will do credit to the force' (RMP Regulations 1931). Thanks to the First World War, a good supply of such men was available on the 'Rosters for Employment of Regular Sailors, Soldiers, and Airmen'. They were sworn in as special constables, but had no authority to act as police, except for military purposes under the Army Act. The RMP was far from a toothless guard dog, however. Applicants were accepted only after replacing substandard teeth with dentures, at their own expense.

Headquarters was at the Admiralty, with area commands at each home port, and at the RN Armament Depot at Crombie in Scotland. Service records were maintained as for the Royal Marines, but at area headquarters rather than divisional. Records for a member of the RMP must be sought, therefore, in both places. Pay and accounts were also decentralized, men being carried on the books of their dockyard, Rosyth in the case of Crombie. A pensioner's old RM Division was notified of his re-enlistment and RMP registration number, the latter being prefixed 'CH/RMP', 'PO/RMP', 'PL/RMP' and 'SC/RMP' as appropriate. The cap badge was the usual Globe and Laurel, but in white metal.

The Second World War placed heavy demands on the RMP, which was supplemented by an RMP Reserve and the Admiralty Civil Police. These were all amalgamated into the Admiralty Constabulary on 2 October 1949, which was itself absorbed into the Ministry of Defence (MoD) Police on 1 October 1971.

1.6 Associated regiments and corps

Military units form ties with other formations for a variety of sentimental and practical reasons. The attitude of the family historian to these will differ from that of a serving or recent member of the formation in question. For example, the modern association of the Royal Marines with the Princess of Wales's Royal Regiment concerns the family historian less than the historical sea service of the ancient regiments now subsumed in the modern regiment. Family historians must also distinguish between ancestors serving in regiments descended from early marine regiments, who may have been marines – depending on when they served – and ancestors who served in regiments employed at sea, but never officially a marine unit. The former may appear in marine records, the latter in army records.

a) Early marine regiments
Most of these were dissolved as discussed in section 1.2.1. The exceptions were four regiments raised in 1704, which transferred to the army. Regiments of

foot were originally known by their numbers within the line. These are shown below, along with the title under which they were known before postwar amalgamations destroyed their old identity, and their current title.

Colonel	Year	Number	Regimental Titles
William Seymour 'Queen's Marines'	1710	4th	1945: King's Own Royal Regt 2007: Duke of Lancaster's Own Regt
Charles Wills	1713	30th	1945: East Lancashire Regt 2007: Duke of Lancaster's Own Regt
Sir Harry Goring	1713	31st	1945: East Surrey Regt 2007: Princess of Wales's Royal Regt
John Bor	1713	32nd	1945: Duke of Cornwall's Light Infantry 2007: Light Infantry*

* The Light Infantry are now retitled unconvincingly as Rifles.

Particular friendship existed between the Royal Marines and East Surreys after Chatham Division cared for survivors of the latter's 1st battalion, who escaped the destruction of the troopship *Kent* by fire in 1825.

The 1740s marine regiments were numbered within the line as 44th to 53rd Foot. The army re-used these numbers after the disbandment of 1748, but none of the new regiments so numbered has any connection with the Royal Marines.

b) Regiments serving as marines

Numerous regiments of foot served as marines until the 1790s, making up the deficiencies of an inadequate and sometimes non-existent marine establishment. The men of these regular infantry units were not recruited as marines, and will not appear in marine records. They should appear in ships' muster lists, but must otherwise be sought in the appropriate army records. The list is compiled from various sources, and may not be complete.

Number	Regimental Titles	Marine Service
1st Guards	Grenadier Guards	1665
2nd Guards	Coldstream Guards	1665
2nd	1945: Queen's Royal Regt 2007: Princess of Wales's Royal Regt	1730, 1781–2, 1785, 1793–5 'Glorious 1st of June'

Number	Regimental Titles	Marine Service
6th	1945: Royal Warwickshire Regt 2007: Royal Regt of Fusiliers	1793–5
7th	1945: Royal Fusiliers 2007: Royal Regt of Fusiliers	1718–20 Cape Passaro 1730; 1756 Minorca
9th	1945: Royal Norfolk Regt 2007: Royal Anglian Regt	1718–20 Cape Passaro
11th	1945: Devonshire Regt 2007: Devonshire and Dorset Regt*	1794–7
12th	1945: Suffolk Regt 2007: Royal Anglian Regt	1718–20 Cape Passaro
14th	1945: West Yorkshire Regt 2007: Yorkshire Regt	1730
15th	1945: East Yorkshire Regt 2007: Yorkshire Regt	1793–5
25th	1945: King's Own Scottish Borderers 2007: Royal Regiment of Scotland	1793–7 'Glorious 1st of June'
27th	1945: Royal Inniskilling Fusiliers 2007: Royal Irish Regt	1718–20 Cape Passaro
29th	1945: Worcestershire Regt 2007: Mercian Regt	1740–2, 1793–5 'Glorious 1st of June'
30th	1945: East Lancashire Regt 2007: Duke of Lancaster's Own Regt	1740–7, 1761–3, 1793–7
34th	1945: Border Regt 2007: Duke of Lancaster's Own Regt	1740
35th	1945: Royal Sussex Regt 2007: Princess of Wales's Royal Regt	1718–20 Cape Passaro
36th	1945: Worcestershire Regt 2007: Mercian Regt	1740
39th	1945: Dorsetshire Regt 2007: Devonshire and Dorset Regt*	1718–20 Cape Passaro 1744–7
49th	1945: Royal Berkshire Regt 2007: Light Infantry*	1801 Copenhagen

Number	Regimental Titles	Marine Service
50th	1945: Royal West Kent Regt 2007: Princess of Wales's Royal Regt	1778 Ushant
53rd	1945: King's Shropshire Light Infantry 2007: Light Infantry*	1790
69th	1945: Welch Regt 2007: Royal Welsh Regt	1782 'The Saintes' 1793–7 'Glorious 1st of June' and Cape St Vincent
95th	1945: Rifle Brigade 2007: Royal Greenjackets*	1801 Copenhagen
98th	1945: North Staffordshire Regt 2007: Mercian Regt	1782

* Light Infantry, Devonshire and Dorsets, and Royal Greenjackets are now re-titled as Rifles.

Some twentieth-century army units have served as or with marines:

- 29 Commando Regiment RA and 59 Independent Commando Squadron RE are an integral part of 3 Commando Brigade RM. Their personnel are commando-trained, and wear the green beret.
- The 2nd battalion Argyll and Sutherland Highlanders (now Royal Regiment of Scotland) formed a composite battalion with survivors of the RM detachments of HMS *Prince of Wales* and *Repulse* at Singapore in 1942, jointly known as the Plymouth Argylls from a football team of the day. The Argylls' 8th battalion also served with the RM Division 1940–1.
- Representatives of numerous regiments served in Army Commandos (see section 1.2.4). No.10 (Inter-Allied) Commando consisted of refugees from occupied Europe. Today's Belgian Paracommando Regiment descends directly from No.4 Troop of that unit.
- The 2nd battalion Duke of Cornwall's Light Infantry provided a marine detachment for the pre-dreadnought battleship HMS *Triumph* when she was mobilized in China in 1914.

c) Modern associations

The Royal Marines celebrate links with the following:

- The Princess of Wales's Royal Regiment includes several regiments who were either raised as marines, or served as such (see above).

- The Royal Netherlands Marine Corps provides part of the joint UK/Netherlands Landing Force with 3 Commando Brigade.
- The United States Marine Corps (USMC) have fought alongside the Royal Marines on numerous occasions, notably during the siege of the Peking Legations in 1900. During the Korean War 41 Independent Commando RM fought under 1st US Marine Division at Chosin Reservoir in November 1950, receiving the US Presidential Citation, the USA's highest unit award.

1.7 Corps mythology

1.7.1 Nicknames

- Bootneck: naval slang for a marine, from the leather stock once worn by all soldiers, hence 'Leatherneck' used of US Marines.
- Joey: contraction of the archaic 'Joe the Marine', as opposed to Jack Tar the sailor.
- Jollies: another obsolete term for marines, originally used of the London Trained Bands, some of whom may have joined the Duke's Regiment in 1664. A private soldier of that regiment named Thomas Jolley became involved in a pub brawl on pledging the Duke of York's health in 1682.
- Lobster: an old nickname for a red-coated soldier, the RMA in blue therefore being 'unboiled' lobsters.
- Royal: unusually polite lower deck slang for a Royal Marine.

1.7.2 Female marines
The persistence and popularity of stories about female soldiers, sailors and marines tell us as much about the human mind as historical reality. The most famous female marine was Hannah Snell, born in 1723, who served as James Gray. She published her exploits in 1750, claiming to have served at sea and the siege of Pondicherry in India. Here she suffered twelve wounds, 'some of which were dangerous', without being discovered. Colonel Cyril Field RMLI unmasked several young women claiming to have served as marines, or attempting to do so: Hannah Witney (1761), Jane Meace (1762) and 'Arthur Douglas' (1757) whose real name is unknown. This chance sample suggests the difficulty female marines present the family historian, who needs both the real name of their adventurous ancestress, and her *nom de guerre*.

1.7.3 Horse Marines
Many derivations have been proposed for the paradoxical notion of a marine on horseback. The literal-minded point to an unfortunate party of 17th Light Dragoons shipped, without horses, in the *Success* or perhaps *Hermione* in 1795.

The practical quote numerous examples of real marines leaping into the saddle, from Java in 1811 to Belize in 1914. The most unlikely mounted detachment was probably the company of Royal Marines who served with the Guards Camel Regiment during the Gordon Relief Expedition of 1885. Etymologists derive the term from a derisive nautical term for a landlubber, or a corruption of 'hawser', something on which early marines often had to pull. Colonel Field attributed the expression to the white horse of Hanover featured on the front flap of the new marines' sugar-loaf caps in 1755. Thus distinguished from their predecessors, whose mitre-caps bore a star, every marine was then a Horse Marine.

Chapter 2

ADMINISTRATION – HOW MARINES ARE MADE

The shape of this chapter reflects the progress of a marine's career. It begins with recruitment, the factors that might influence a decision to join the Corps, and the rewards and punishments that governed behaviour thereafter. It describes the clothing and equipment delineating the marine's outward form, and the barrack life and training that prepared him inwardly for service. The main published source for Royal Marine administration is *King's Regulations and Admiralty Instructions* for various years. Wall and Ritson's *Royal Marine Pocket Book* gives a good idea of 1940s 'interior economy' (see Further Reading). Chapter 3 will discuss the types of operation a marine might subsequently experience, and conclude by considering how a marine's career might end.

2.1 Sources of manpower

Military organizations need manpower. How they satisfy that need depends on the society from which they spring. Britain's armed forces traditionally reflected the class structure of British society, with a clear division between commissioned and other ranks, which has only recently begun to break down. The distinction between the few and the many recur throughout this chapter.

2.1.1 Recruitment of other ranks
Recruitment of early marines was the task of regimental officers authorized by Royal Warrant to raise volunteers by beat of drum. Wartime parliaments allowed conscription 'of such able bodied men as are not younger than 17, nor more than 45, nor papists, nor less than 5ft 4ins high, and having no vote for parliament men, and, who do not exercise any lawful calling or employment'. Otherwise, recruiting officers depended on volunteers driven by hunger, befuddled with drink or lured by bounties. John Brooks got £4 12s 6d when he enlisted in 1803, several months wages for an agricultural labourer.

Well-armed members of the Royal Marine Artillery Cadet Corps about 1900, wearing the slouch hats made popular by the Boer War.

Recruiting parties consisted of an officer, sergeant, drummer and several reliable men, preferably acquainted with the recruitment area. From 1786 Chatham Division took the eastern counties, from Kent to Northumberland; Plymouth the west from Cornwall and Devon to Cumberland; Portsmouth the south and centre, from Hampshire to Staffordshire. London and the populous manufacturing districts were never closed to any division. Allocations were not watertight, however. John Brooks, who enlisted in Bristol, joined a Chatham company.

Most early marines came from society's lower ranks, though not necessarily its dregs. John Brooks was a cooper and a skilled man. Portsmouth description books suggest most marine recruits were agricultural labourers (48 per cent), or textile workers (18 per cent). The remainder followed every trade, including bakers, builders, carpenters, glass cutters, hairdressers and wheelwrights. One surprising source of recruits was prisoners of war, desperate to escape the hulks in Portsmouth Harbour. Another was runaway slaves, who formed three companies of 'Colonial Marines' at Tangier Island in Chesapeake Bay in 1814 to fight their old masters. After the war they received land in Trinidad, where some of their descendants still live.

Meeting physical standards was difficult. A newspaper described a deserter from the Duke's as 'a squat, bow-legged squinting fellow and almost blind of one eye, aged about 30'. Poor quality recruits inspired a flood of naval complaint in the 1740s: 'very indifferent weak poor creatures, some being boys and the others decayed old men unfit to serve their country.' Some were 'so infected with the Itch [scabies] that it would be madness to send them aboard'. Even healthy marines were small. The French at the siege of Belle Isle in 1761 described them as 'Petits Grenadiers'. Major John Pitcairn, commanding a battalion at Boston, Massachusetts, in 1775, found his marines shorter than regular infantrymen, and argued for a minimum height of 5ft 6ins.

Reduced demand for manpower and improved nutrition solved the problem. Victorian marines were second only to guardsmen in stature. Minimum requirements for the RMLI in 1915 were 5ft 7ins, 6/6 vision, normal colour vision and educational attainments equivalent to boy seamen. RMA gunners had to be 5ft 9ins. Second or third generation marines were common. Boy Bugler C A Smith followed father and uncle into the Corps, at the turn of the twentieth century. He quickly recovered from homesickness, and even liked the corporal, a family history that challenges common views of the horrors of service life.

The First World War brought short service enlistment for the conflict's duration, and eventually conscription. From January 1916 a proportion of recruits destined for the RND came from the army pool at Reading, although voluntary enlistment continued for long and short service marines. Walter Popham volunteered rather than risk being conscripted, thinking the Royal Marines 'a better Corps than some'. The Second World War brought further compulsion, with some conscripts choosing to serve as 'Hostilities Only' or 'HO' Marines. National service ended in 1963, since when all Royal Marines have enlisted under voluntary engagements.

Enlistment produces some of the most useful records for family history. Attestations from 1755 onwards provide personal details unavailable anywhere else for working-class people of the period. John Brooks was 5ft 3ins

ROYAL MARINES.

An opportunity now offers for

SPIRITED YOUNG MEN

To Enlist in that truly

LOYAL AND GALLANT CORPS,

IN WHICH GOOD CONDUCT IS

CERTAIN OF ITS REWARD;

WHEN EMBARKED THEY HAVE

GREAT ADVANTAGES,

They may see almost every Foreign Nation in the World, and have excellent living at the same time, consisting of Beef, Plumb Pudding, and a **Pint of Grog** daily, or Wine in proportion.

A chance of **PRIZE MONEY**, besides having the great satisfaction of upholding their Country's Honor; and on their return after about three years absence, they will be enabled to see their Friends with **Pockets** well lined, or to purchase their **Discharge** if they should not wish to remain in the service.

THE BOUNTY IS £3 17 6

GOD SAVE THE QUEEN.

As the number required will soon be filled up, an early application is recommended, to SERJEANT   *Rendezvous*

at the

R. RIXON, Printer, Bookseller, and Stationer, Woolwich.

Victorian recruiting poster c. 1842 explaining the benefits of enlistment. The location and date of the recruiting party's visit would be written in the space at the bottom.

tall, had fair hair and a fresh complexion. The data was copied into description books, many of which survive, filling the gaps where original loose sheets have disappeared.

2.1.2 Commissioned officers

The entry of young gentlemen as commissioned officers differed in every way from recruitment of the common marine. Early marine officers bought their commissions, like army officers. Purchase had much to recommend it. It produced a socially coherent officer class, disinclined to rock the political boat. On retirement officers could cash in their investment, saving parliament having to fund proper pensions.

Cheap marine commissions reflected the instability of marine regiments, and the consequent risk of losing one's investment. A lieutenancy of marines could be had for £200–£250 before 1755, compared with £350–£400 in an old marching regiment. The system's abuses were moderated in various ways. Promotion went by regimental seniority, so that a vacant captaincy was offered to existing lieutenants first, excluding well-heeled outsiders. Marine regiments raised in 1739 were commanded by old officers, their captains, 'Gentlemen of Service taken from Half pay . . . or Subalterns of long standing'.

Purchase into the marines ended in 1755. It conflicted with the Royal Navy's officer selection procedures, and hindered wartime expansion. Future marine officers would be appointed through the 'interest' of influential friends or, as Colonel Field put it, 'partiality, favour and affection'. Thomas Marmaduke Wybourn obtained his commission through the patronage of Earl Spencer, First Lord of the Admiralty. Abuses of the system were again moderated by practice. John MacIntire, a marine subaltern of the 1760s, thought 'Interest can procure a Commission, [but] Education and Good Conduct constitute the Gentleman'. Lord St Vincent felt, 'the requests of fatherless children and widows cannot be parried', and limited his patronage to officers' sons and near relations.

Qualifications beyond social status were limited. John Tatton Brown, later a general, 'passed examination before My Lords Commissioners of the Admiralty', but did not say in what subjects. The headmaster of Lewis Roteley, who fought at Trafalgar, thought him 'capable of any Situation where Writing and Accounting only are necessary'. By the 1840s candidates for marine commissions faced examination in arithmetic, algebra, trigonometry and logarithms. When the army abolished purchase in 1871, it instituted competitive examinations, in which the RMLI and RMA participated, passing into the Royal Military College at Sandhurst or Woolwich Academy respectively. The Selborne Scheme of 1902 imposed a single entry system on all candidates for naval commissions, whether as executive, engineer or marine officers, but this was never popular with the latter. Aspirant marines continued to take a Sandhurst type of examination before studying at Greenwich Naval College.

Officers of marines were rarely aristocrats. The life was too uncertain and prospects too dim. Indeed it is unclear what did motivate young men of good family to pursue a career in the marines. Most came from the untitled gentry or the professional classes, eighteenth-century commissions identifying them as 'esquire' rather than 'gentleman'. The father of Arthur Tooker Collins, who died a general, was a bookseller. Many were sons of clergymen. Often commissions ran in families. The Duke's Regiment was stuffed with Cornish gentry: Killigrews, Wrays and Trelawneys. Generations of marine officers shared such names as Adair, Collins, Elliot, Halliday, Oldfield or Pitcairn. Many eighteenth-century officers were Scottish, as the Union opened up prospects for ambitious Scots of superior education.

The First World War brought commissions for 'temporary gentlemen'. Most came from university or public school, others from the Inns of Court Officer Training Corps, preserving the social status quo. Later the RMLI replaced RND officer casualties from the army's officer cadet battalions, opening the door to regular soldiers from lower social classes. Others came up through the Corps. Pre-war warrant officers and NCOs were promoted lieutenant, not only as quartermasters, the traditional aspiration of the long service soldier, but as platoon commanders. The Second World War saw further erosion of the class basis of officer cadres as an increasing proportion of Royal Marine officers were commissioned from the ranks.

Officers' careers are both simpler and more difficult to trace than those of other ranks. An alphabetical list of officers of marines whose service records have survived for 1793–1970 is available at the National Archives in ADM 313/110 and on the open shelves. However, service records are incomplete before 1837. Little personal information appears in the first printed seniority lists of 1767, or the Army and Navy Lists that appear from 1740 and 1797 respectively. Nineteenth-century Navy Lists are more helpful, listing officers alphabetically, by seniority and by ship, and describing their meritorious services. Commissions, promotions and resignations appeared in the monthly *London Gazette*, which is indexed from the nineteenth century. Information concerning more recently appointed officers must be sought from the Ministry of Defence.

2.2 Terms of service

The literal meaning of 'soldier' is a man who serves for pay. Money was an essential part of the government's bargain with the enlisted marine, and still more so his officers. Regular pay was just one element in the package. There was the glittering promise of prize money, rather like winning the lottery, and the daily promise of food and drink, something not guaranteed to every labouring man in the eighteenth century. Before paid holidays became common, there was some entitlement to leave, and, for officers, insurance against unemployment in the shape of half-pay.

2.2.1 Pay

Rates of pay were low, even by the standards of pre-industrial Britain. A soldier of the Duke's Regiment was due eight old pence a day, a penny less than the wages of a contemporary ploughman. The value of this meagre sum was eroded throughout the eighteenth century until wartime inflation drove the fleet, including its marines, to mutiny in 1797. The first pay rise for over a century brought the private marine's daily wage to the proverbial shilling a day, supplemented in 1806 by an additional penny or twopence a day after seven or fourteen years' service. An RMLI private still received 1s 2d in the 1890s, when an unskilled labourer earned nearly three shillings a day. The RMA did better, being paid as Royal Artillerymen. Postwar pay increases took a 1920s Royal Marine to 4s 6d for a trained man with six years' service. Sergeants received 1s 6d a day before 1797, 1s 10d in 1806, and 7s 0d after the First World War.

A marine's pay was reduced by various stoppages. Seventeenth-century soldiers paid 'off-reckonings' of twopence a day towards their uniforms and equipment, a sort of hire purchase. The rest of their wages counted as 'subsistence', that is, food and lodgings. Later marines had to buy cleaning materials and 'necessaries', such as the checked shirts worn at sea. The surgeon took twopence a month and the chaplain four pence. Sixpence a month went to Greenwich Hospital and the Chatham Chest, a sort of insurance fund for disabled sailors. Many marines incurred debts, taking part-time jobs to pay them off.

Poor administration exacerbated matters for the early regiments. Marine officers starved, while their men threatened to pull down the Navy Board Office unless they were paid. If money was available, regimental musters were impossible at sea, causing endless delay. Twelve years after Shovell's Marines had disbanded in 1697, the Treasury finally authorized payment of two lieutenants, incorrectly certified as dead.

Payment issues were largely resolved after 1755, marines always being paid on embarking and landing. They received at least half their back pay on disembarkation, less the cost of any clothing or tobacco bought from the purser. If new clothing failed to materialize they got the cash instead. By the 1840s the government issued kit *gratis*, men being charged only for damage or loss. Nineteenth-century marines went to sea for three years, and swaggered home to their village with a pocketful of money. Wild scenes attended paying off, as might be expected among men receiving £40 or £80 after months at sea. Two privates paid off from HMS *Pluto* in 1847 began eating their £5 notes with bread, cheese and onions, but were stopped in time.

Embarkation pay was especially important before the navy introduced dependants' allowances. Previously families of marines sent overseas had faced starvation. Jane Dyer, 'under sentence of death for a bare felony', petitioned for her life in 1705 as the only support of two children, whose father Cornelius Dyer was at Gibraltar in Bor's Marine Regiment. From 1792 a marine could allocate some of his pay to his family, from 10s 6d a month for a private to £1 1s for a sergeant. During the Second World War a man might allot six sevenths of his pay, which the payee then drew from the post office on producing their allotment book. Children's allowances were paid regardless of their parents' marital status, provided these were living together.

Marine officers had less authority at sea than naval officers, but were better paid. One Victorian officer is said to have asked where else could he get so much money for doing so little. Rates in 1806 ranged from 5s 3d a day for a second lieutenant to £2 for a colonel commandant, rising to 10s 0d and £3 10s respectively in the 1920s. Adjutants and quartermasters received extra, as did wireless telegraphy assistants who received a shilling a day in 1913, rising to 2s 6d on their qualifying as instructors. While other ranks were paid every twenty-eight days, officers received their money every three lunar months, or eighty-four days. Pay and accounting records do exist for the marines, but at summary levels, without detail of individual payments.

2.2.2 Prize money

Recruiting posters made much of the marine's brilliant prospects, 'When every Thing that swims the Seas must be a PRIZE!'. Sergeant John Howe was moved to join by folk memories of Spanish gold, perhaps from the treasure ship *Hermione* taken in 1762, when every private marine present got £484. His own best effort was £11 8s from a shipload of wine. Prize money was usually awarded for enemy ships, but also for captured cities. Marines present at the siege of Havana in 1762 received £4 1s 8d apiece.

Marines shared prize money on the same basis as seamen from 1692. The system was biased in favour of the officers, particularly the ship's captain. Shares in force throughout the great age of prize, between the Marlborough and Napoleonic Wars, were one-eighth to the commander-in-chief, a quarter to the captain, one-eighth to the master and lieutenants, one to the warrant officers, one to the petty officers and marine sergeants, and a quarter to the lower deck, including marine corporals, privates and drummers. Captains of marines counted as naval lieutenants, subalterns as naval warrant officers.

Prize money could be lucrative. Captain John Robyns RM reckoned the *Seahorse* took £100,000 in prizes on the eastern American seaboard in 1814. Officers used all their influence to be posted to a frigate with its superior prospects of prize money. Lewis Roteley claimed he was passed over three times in this way. Eventually he paid £10 for another officer's place on the roster to embark in a frigate bound for the West Indies. Subsequent experience was discouraging. Captured ships were released as neutrals, or sold off cheaply. The prize court was 'a den of rogues', while his Trafalgar prize money fell far short of expectations.

Years could elapse before money was paid out. The *London Gazette, Navy List* and periodicals like the *Gentleman's Magazine* advertised payments due to a particular ship, without naming claimants. Queen Victoria's colonial wars accrued prize money, but never on the Napoleonic scale. Small amounts were paid after the First and Second World Wars.

2.2.3 *Rations and allowances*
The sailing navy's awful food is the stuff of legend. Mahogany beef and weevilly bread are only part of the story, however. Marines ashore were fed better than many civilians; rations at sea were not always good, but they were plentiful.

Marines at sea were fed as seamen. A recruiting poster of 1812 listed the daily allowance as an inducement to enlist, directly after sixteen guineas' bounty: 1lb of beef or pork and another of bread, with flour, raisins, butter, cheese, oatmeal, molasses, tea and sugar. Individuals acquired green vegetables where they could, robbing prizes, foraging ashore or trading tobacco. Scurvy remained a menace until the introduction of a lime or lemon juice ration during the 1790s. Salt beef and hard tack became curiosities in the twentieth century, replaced by corned beef sandwiches. Steamships condensed fresh water, baked their own bread and stored frozen meat.

Rations ashore were more varied. Arthur Tooker Collins's notebook lists dinner menus in the 1740s: mutton and broth, bacon and greens, beef and pudding, fried beef and roots. The daily ration per man in barracks during the 1830s was ¾lb of meat and 1½lb of bread, supplemented by local vegetables. This provided two meals a day, as in the army. Men bought the makings of a third meal privately, or from 'Wet' and 'Dry' canteens that sold beer or groceries. Breakfast and tea consisted of dry bread known as 'slingers', and tea boiled up in dixies used for stew. Food improved in the 1890s, with extra pay for sergeant cooks. Bugler Smith left a glowing account of military cuisine:

Roast beef thick batter pudding fine greens and excellent new potatoes, one of my favourite dinners, but how about Sunday, boiled pork, broad beans, potatoes, and gippa . . . afterwards we had a huge cherry pie about 2ft 6ins long and 2ft wide and 6ins deep . . . the only fault was that when you had finished your mouth and teeth were as black as ink.

In the Second World War a general messing system provided four meals a day, using ingredients acquired wholesale, and prepared by qualified cooks. RM Divisions allowed 18s 9d a day per man, plus 2s 5d extra per recruit under 18 years. Married men living ashore could claim Victualling Allowance of 1s 11½d a day, while personnel in lodgings, like the early commandos, could receive a combined Lodgings and Provision Allowance of 3s 6d.

There was, for a long time, a cash relationship between a marine's rations and his pay. Soldiers of the Duke's Regiment were stopped 1¼d a day for their bread. A 1790s private paid four shillings a week for messing. Food was free at sea, but pay reduced: from 8d to 6d before 25 July 1797, and from 1s to 8d afterwards. Not until 1854 were marines paid the same at sea as ashore, where in 1904 rations finally became free. Grog money (21s a quarter in 1945) was paid in lieu of the daily ration of 1/8 pint of spirits, which was not issued at the depot and divisions.

A major gain of the Spithead mutiny was abolition of short weight, an abuse by which the ship's purser issued 14oz in the pound, a saving to him of one seventh. This was not the same as short allowance, by which seamen and marines received extra pay when rations were reduced for operational reasons, for example six men sharing four men's rations. John Howe went on short rations in 1780: ¼lb bread and ¼lb rice, the beef very bad, no butter, cheese or flour.

Officers generally fed better. Lewis Rotely wrote home about the capital dinners in the *Victory*, estimating his mess bills at £50–£60 a year. Besides laying in 'stock' such as port wine and live sheep, officers sampled breadfruit, ostrich pancakes, dolphin 'dry eating' and turtle. Lieutenant Henry Woodruff's cabin on leaving Rio de Janeiro in 1855 resembled a greengrocer's. The wardroom was not exempt from the exigencies of the service, however. Thomas Wybourn went on short allowance in 1803 with everyone else, 'the bread full of vermin and musty – but the greatest misfortune was want of water . . . only one pint a day for these last five weeks, and this was so bad sometimes, as to oblige us to hold our *noses* while drinking'.

2.2.4 Leave, furlough and half-pay
Early marines could legitimately be absent from duty for three reasons. An individual might be granted leave of absence for a period for some specific

reason, such as compassionate leave. One or more marines might receive furlough on return from sea service, in modern terms a holiday. Officers might go on half-pay, sometimes for personal reasons, more usually as a government economy measure.

The nature and duration of leave was different for commissioned and other ranks. Officers were men of substance with affairs to see to; other ranks rarely had a home outside the corps. Divisional orders refer to officers receiving leave of absence for two weeks or a month, sometimes renewed for another month. Other ranks were more likely to receive a pass for the evening. Married men might sleep out of barracks, no more than three per company in the 1770s. Regulations aboard the *Royal George* in 1812 allowed land absence 'as far as circumstances permit', but never more than twenty-four hours without the captain's permission. Railways made it easier to return home for short periods. Twentieth-century marine diarists refer to frequent trips home; there was leave at Christmas, or while ships were in dry dock.

Overnight leave was a reward for good behaviour. Captains of ships were instructed to defer to their OCRM when granting leave, giving the latter a rare sanction against defaulters. Only the 'best and soberest' men were allowed to lie out of barracks in the 1770s. A century later NCOs and men with Good Conduct Badges (GCB) might stay out overnight twice a week. Furlough was more substantial. Portsmouth division allowed up to three men on furlough per company in the 1760s, on application through their company commander. Later, furlough was in proportion to sea service. Marines returning to RMA headquarters in the 1870s were due fourteen days after less than a year at sea, rising to fifty-six days after four years away. The 1940s saw various leave allowances, depending where a man was serving, besides long or short weekend leave granted by COs, general holidays like the king's birthday, re-engaging and pension leave.

Half-pay was at once a grievance and a safety net. It was a retainer for officers who might be recalled to duty, allowing the Admiralty to preserve a cadre of experienced officers. Until 1791 it was also the only form of pension for officers no longer fit for service, and a way of punishing the recalcitrant. Half-pay was paid until an officer died, or was otherwise provided for. Reduced officers were expected to remain on call, but many took other jobs, purchasing commissions in line regiments or the East India Company's forces. Eusebius Sylvester risked his health as well as his half-pay, becoming an 'Agent to Sennigambia in Africa'.

Half-pay was better than it sounds. A lieutenant of seven years' standing in the 1840s was due 4s 6d a day compared with 7s 6d on duty, that is, 60 per cent rather than 50 per cent. A half-pay colonel was due 14s 6d, paid quarterly. Incomplete records exist at the National Archives of half-pay paid following peace dividends in the 1760s and late 1810s, not always under ADM references. An 1816 Address Book of Reduced Officers seems a particularly useful source. Half-pay persisted into the twentieth century, the Pay Master General's records (PMG 15) covering 1836 to 1920.

2.3 Rewards and discipline

The marine hierarchy employed various motivational tools beyond the everyday compensations of pay and rations. Some measures were positive, such as the use of medals or promotions to encourage the deserving. Less desirable behaviour might face punitive sanctions.

2.3.1 Medals and awards

Medals provide some of the most tangible and moving evidence of an ancestor's life. Specialists distinguish between orders, decorations and medals, in descending order of prestige. They also speak of 'gallantry awards'. For most practical purposes the term 'medal' is sufficient. Those wishing to know more should consult Connolly (*Spink's Guide*) and Spencer (*Medals – The Researcher's Guide*), both in Further Reading. Military medals fall into four groups:

1. Awards for gallantry in action, the supreme example being the Victoria Cross (VC).
2. Active service medals for whole wars or specific campaigns, e.g. the South Atlantic Medal awarded for the Falklands War in 1982.
3. Efficiency or long service decorations.
4. Commemorative awards, such as the Coronation Medal of 1953, or the Jubilee Medal of 1977.

Most medals are shaped like a cross, star or circle, cast in bronze, silver or cupro-nickel bronze. They carry a design on the front and back, which are known as the 'obverse' and 'reverse'. Details of the recipient are often engraved around the edge or on the reverse. British medals usually hang from a coloured ribbon with a pattern specific to the medal. Strips of metal mounted on the ribbon are either a 'clasp', identifying an action or campaign, or a 'bar' indicating a further award of the same medal. As part of the Royal Navy, Royal Marines receive naval medals, except when serving ashore as an integral part of the army.

Medals are, with few exceptions, a Victorian invention. The first official award to junior ranks of the Royal Marines was the Naval General Service Medal 1793–1840 (NGSM). Issued in 1848, it had 230 possible bars, starting with Lord Howe's victory of '1st June 1794', known as the 'Glorious First of June'. The final bar was 'Syria', for operations in November 1840. Douglas-Morris lists recipients in *Naval Medals 1793–1856*. Specific campaign awards followed with medals for the Crimea and Baltic, both 1854–6, the Indian Mutiny 1857–8, and China 1857–60. Royal Marines were eligible for all these. A few also received the Ashantee Medal 1873–4 for operations on the Gold Coast. This evolved into the East and West Africa Medal 1887–1900 with numerous clasps for landings by naval brigades (see section 3.1.2). A later NGSM recognized minor operations between 1915 and 1962.

The Victoria Cross, first and most celebrated of gallantry awards, was instituted in 1856. Three Royal Marines won VCs during the Crimean War, and all ten Royal Marine VCs are displayed at the Royal Marines Museum. The Crimean War also saw the first issue of the Conspicuous Gallantry Medal (CGM) to RN personnel, including Royal Marine NCOs and other ranks. The

A common group of First World War medals, from left to right: the bronze 1914 star, silver British War Medal, and yellow bronze Victory Medal, known derisively as 'Pip, Squeak, & Wilfred'. The bar on the 1914 star indicates the recipient served in France or Belgium in 1914. This group were issued to Pte George Harwood RMLI.

First World War saw further gallantry awards with the Distinguished Service Medal (DSM) open to seamen and marines. Royal Marines serving on the Western Front from 1916 could also receive the Military Cross (MC) for officers, or the Military Medal (MM) for other ranks, and the Distinguished Conduct Medal (DCM), the CGM's military equivalent. Today all ranks are eligible for the MC when fighting ashore.

Generic medals were issued to very many veterans in both World Wars. The First World War produced the British War Medal, the Victory Medal and the much coveted 1914 Star, often and wrongly called the 'Mons Star'.

Royal Marines who landed at Ostend and Antwerp in 1914 were eligible for this. H E Blumberg lists the War Medal's naval clasps in *Britain's Sea Soldiers 1914–1919*, along with British and foreign decorations issued to Royal Marines 1914–18.

The Second World War produced the Defence Medal 1939–45, the 1939–45 War Medal, and the 1939–45 Star. It also saw specific campaign medals: the Atlantic, Africa, Pacific, Burma, Italy, and France and Germany Stars with distinctive ribbons. Possession of one or more of these may suggest where a

A group of Second World War medals, including an OBE and British Empire Medal (to the left). They were issued to Major Arthur Ebsworth RM. Unlike the First World War medals, the 1939–45 counterparts were not named. The oakleaf attached to the 1939–45 War Medal indicates he was 'mentioned in despatches'.

Royal Marine served. A holder of an Italy Star, for example, might have served in 7th Battalion, or else in 40, 41, or 43 RM Commando.

Medals for good behaviour appeared in the nineteenth century as a more positive form of motivation than physical punishment. The Long Service and Good Conduct Medal (LSGCM) was introduced in 1831, for Royal Marine NCOs and men who had served fifteen years with continuous 'very good' character on their Company Conduct and/or Service Sheets. The Meritorious Service Medal (MSM) was introduced to the Royal Marines in 1849, for sergeants or above after twenty-one years' service.

Some medals also conferred material benefits. The CGM and DCM were worth £20 on discharge or promotion. An annuity of up to £20 a year accompanied the MSM. LSGCM holders earned a gratuity in proportion to service after its award. The basic rate in 1913 was £1 per year until retirement, with a maximum of £5. NCOs could accumulate more, as tabulated in *Admiralty Instructions*. These varied, so it is worth checking the edition in force for a particular ancestor. Good Conduct Badges, introduced in 1833 for all marines below warrant officer were worth a penny a day for each one awarded, up to six in 1913, only three in the 1940s.

The best starting point when researching gallantry or meritorious service awards is the announcement in the *London Gazette*. Sometimes these are accompanied by a citation describing the circumstances of the award. More often the recommendation leading to the award was not published, but kept at the National Archives. Obituary notices in *The Times* or *Globe & Laurel* can be helpful, as may lists of gallantry awards compiled by medal collectors. Campaign medals awarded to Royal Marines up to 1920 are recorded in alphabetical order in Royal Naval Medal Rolls. Details of army gallantry medals awarded during the First World War, however, will be in army records, foreign decorations in Foreign Office records. Admiralty records exist for the LSGCM from 1849 to 1894. Douglas-Morris's *The Naval Long Service Medals* is also useful.

2.3.2 Promotion and commissions from the ranks
Armed forces, unlike commercial organizations, staff their senior levels by internal promotion. This achieves three purposes: it creates a command structure imbued with the methods and traditions of the service; it rewards the successful; and encourages the ambitious. Before the First World War, promotion in the Royal Marines reflected British class divisions, with separate career structures for commissioned and other ranks. Few of the latter ever gained a commission. As for commissioned officers, their anomalous position as soldiers within a naval service exerted a malign influence over their chances and speed of promotion.

The marine rank structure is outlined in the preface. Starting at the bottom, a recruit would join as a private, or since 1923 as a marine. A few began as drummers, or later as boy buglers. Most left the service as private marines. An expanded wartime company in 1806 had eight sergeants, eight corporals, three drummers and 173 privates, so one man in ten might become an NCO. Military manuals dwelt upon NCOs being sober, neat, honest, not in debt and expert in drill. A sergeant's duties also required him to be literate, and to keep his distance from his erstwhile comrades. Such men played a vital role in the routine operation of the Corps.

Eighteenth-century marines were promoted on the authority of their commanding officer. Portsmouth Division's order books rarely justify promotions. They do, however, give reasons for disratings – usually drink – though one sergeant was demoted for behaving in an 'Infamous and Scandalous Manner', a corporal for bringing in a recruit 'in such a filthy state as to be unfit to appear', and another for cruelty to a prisoner in the black hole. Such notices, however unfortunate, have the advantage for the family historian of naming names. By the end of the nineteenth century the process was less arbitrary. Ambitious marines applied for promotion to corporal, their names appearing on the divisional candidate's roster maintained by the adjutant, and sat written examinations. During the First World War the Corps developed junior leaders in a more deliberate manner, with six week courses at Deal, a practice continued in the Second.

Sea service often required marines to take responsibility above their substantive rating. Corporal John Howe was acting sergeant in *Sceptre* for two years in the 1790s. Temporary NCOs drew the pay for their acting rank, and wore the appropriate chevrons when these were introduced. Captains of ships could delay promotion of NCOs, but not disrate them without the Admiralty's consent. NCOs showing themselves unfit for their position while at sea might be investigated by a captain or Commander RN and two RM officers, and recommended for demotion if found incompetent.

Few NCOs made the step to lieutenant before the twentieth century. They would have lacked the financial means and social skills to enjoy an officer's life, while a senior NCO was of more consequence than any subaltern. Colour Sergeant Walter Gillies was promoted lieutenant for heroic leadership on the Moroccan coast in 1846, but retired immediately. The common route to commissioned rank was in an administrative capacity. As in the army, Royal Marine quartermasters were promoted from senior NCOs. In this respect the Corps was ahead of the Royal Navy, where promotion for lower rates during the nineteenth century was non-existent. It took two world wars to make promotion a regular proposition for men entering the forces on the ground floor.

Promotion prospects for eighteenth- and early nineteenth-century marine officers were poor. A second lieutenant might be promoted after eighteen months to three years, but the step to captain took another twelve to fifteen years. Another fifteen might elapse before reaching major, the best most officers could expect. There were several reasons for this situation: the Royal Navy's stranglehold on preferment, promotion by seniority, and an un-balanced establishment with masses of wartime subalterns competing for a handful of posts above captain.

Naval despatches rarely mentioned marine officers. Only one was promoted after Trafalgar. Bad tempered letters to *The Times* from hard done-by officers RM punctuated almost every nineteenth-century campaign. For a time the Royal Navy even took senior marine posts for itself. 'Blue Colonels' collected forty shillings a day for doing nothing from 1760 until the abuse was abolished in 1833. Promotions after Jutland in 1916 contrasted with earlier neglect, with five RM officers promoted and two RM gunners commissioned as lieutenants.

The move from purchase to promotion by seniority was disastrous for the vitality of the marines, as it was for other seniority corps such as the Royal Artillery. Lacking a pension, elderly officers clung on to their commissions, blocking younger more energetic men. A lieutenant killed at Bunker Hill in 1775 had thirty-six years' service and nine children, the eldest a lieutenant in the Corps. Wholesale reductions after every war created frightful delays. All seventy-five captains heading the list in 1845 had been commissioned over thirty years before. In 1849 two second commandants were aged 67 and 68. Compulsory retirements and promotion by examination improved matters in the later nineteenth century, but promotion remained slow until the First World War.

One consequence of slow promotion was the flight of ambitious officers, who sought advancement elsewhere, however improbable. A half-pay second lieutenant RM was gazetted riding master in the 15th Hussars in 1831. General Sir George Aston who formed the RND had worked in the Naval Intelligence Department. The RND's second commander, General Paris, served with the Rhodesia Field Force in 1900, continuing a trend set by marine special service officers commanding Fanti levies on the Gold Coast, or who joined the Egyptian Camel Corps.

2.3.3 Crime and punishment

Marines were subject to two disciplinary codes, depending where they were. At sea they were 'entitled to the same advantages, and . . . subject to the same discipline as the rest of the ship's company', under the Naval Discipline Act. The same was true of naval shore establishments and RM detachments ashore,

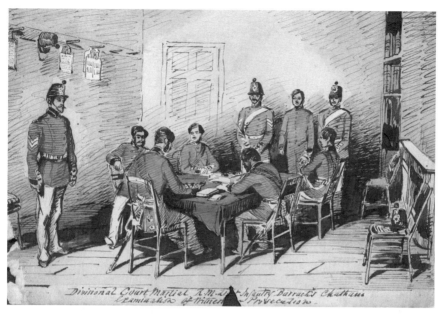

Divisional Court Martial at Chatham painted in the 1860s by Lieutenant Colonel W Masters RMLI. An NCO is giving evidence to the officers around the table, while prisoner and escort stand in the background.

unless the senior naval officer declared that the current Army or Marine Mutiny Act should apply. In that case the marines in question came under military law like land-based soldiers. While at sea and under naval law, marines might still be liable under the Marine Mutiny Act for offences not recognized by naval courts martial. In that case they faced trial at headquarters, in the same way as when they were not embarked in HM ships. Today Royal Marines are subject only to the Naval Discipline Act, wherever they might be.

Divisional courts martial resembled their regimental equivalent in the army, consisting of five officers, presided over by a captain. Intended to deal promptly with minor crimes, they kept no formal records, and submitted their decisions to the colonel commandant for approval. The accused could request a general court martial presided over by an externally appointed judge advocate. Members of the court were sworn, evidence taken on oath and the sentence subject to Admiralty approval. There was no guarantee, however, that a fairer trial would be more lenient.

As soon as a marine detachment went on board ship, however, its officers lost their right to discipline their own men. Naval commanding officers could delegate their extensive powers of punishment only to their second-in-command, namely, another naval officer. Naval discipline lacked even the primitive checks and balances of a military court martial, where commanding officers reviewed decisions, and might exercise clemency. John Howe fell victim to arbitrary naval proceedings in 1782. An unsupported witness picked him out with another man: 'the Lieut would not allow me or any other person to Speak in my be half . . . And next day we were brought to the Gangway but was not allowd to speak in our own behalf and was punished with a Dozen Lashes each' (*sic*). Naval officers also employed considerable incidental violence against the lower deck, not always a wise approach with armed men. In 1712 a marine sentinel snapped his musket at a midshipman who had boxed his ears, 'but by providence it only flashed in ye pan'. By contrast, divisional regulations exhorted officers and NCOs to behave humanely, insisting 'no Man to be struck with Hand or Stick on any Account'.

Even ashore, however, eighteenth-century marines suffered savage punishments. One of Pitcairn's battalion at Boston in 1775 received 800 lashes for insolence and striking an officer. Another got 500 for stealing clothes, and one was hanged for burning fences as firewood – all under an officer who detested corporal punishment, and whose death at Bunker Hill inspired the cry 'We have all lost a father'. Part of the problem was the incorrigible reck-lessness of men who preferred confinement in the 'black hole' on bread and water to doing duty, and who learned nothing from earlier scrapes. John Howe escaped flogging for sleeping at his post, but subsequently received 225, 300 and 400 lashes for selling his own and other people's clothing to buy drink. The mutinies of 1797 added thought crime to charge sheets, one of *Diadem*'s detachment receiving 200 lashes and six months in the Marshalsea prison for a letter to his divisional commandant 'calculated to stir up a disturbance in the ship'.

The most terrible penalties targeted desertion and cowardice in action. John Goodman, a marine in the *Trusty*, was court-martialled and hanged in 1800 'for robbing his ship's stores, quitting his post [as a sentinel], and running away with the ship's boat'. Captain Henry Ruffane was sentenced to be shot after hiding in the *Elisabeth*'s hold during a desperate single ship action in 1745. Executions, as with all punishments, were the occasion of solemn ritual, calculated to impress those paraded to watch. The well-known engraving of Admiral Byng's execution in 1757 shows a firing party of nine marines in three ranks. While the front two give fire with their bayonets nearly touching the unfortunate admiral, the third rank hold their muskets upright, reserving their fire for the *coup de grâce*. Punishment was not always so severe. A corporal and private who deserted from HMS *Juste* in 1800 while employed in Portsmouth dockyard received just fifty lashes, 'in consideration of their good characters'. Lesser offences attracted lesser penalties: pay was stopped to buy needles and thread for tatty marines; coats turned inside out for un-soldierlike behaviour; grog and leave stopped for the uproarious or the tardy.

Physical correction became unacceptable after the Napoleonic Wars, within and outside the service. The Defaulter's Book for HMS *Hastings*'s RM detachment for 1849–53 shows only two men suffering four dozen lashes. One had been frequently drunk, concealed spirits in an officer's chest, urinated on the gangway while sentry and knowingly received stolen bottles of wine. More usual punishments were facing the ship's side, loss of smoking time or watered down grog. In 1859 the Admiralty limited punishment to forty-eight lashes and to persistent offenders only. Both services had suspended flogging by 1871, although it remained in *Admiralty Instructions*. Financial penalties and humiliation replaced corporal punishment. In the early twentieth century Nathaniel Hiscock spent three days carrying shingle along Deal beach for swearing, and worried about losing his Good Conduct Badge after a spectacular drinking session at Vladivostock. The Admiralty now recognized the right of a ship's OCRM to attend disciplinary proceedings against his men, and provide moral and practical support. Marines of all ranks colluded to resolve disciplinary issues amongst themselves.

Troublemakers are always better documented than the well behaved. The names of early marine officers facing courts martial may be found in the indexes of the printed *Calendars of State Papers Domestic*. These in turn point to fuller accounts in the original papers. Official court martial records for the eighteenth and nineteenth centuries hold naval and marine personnel together, officers separate from lesser rates. Nineteenth century registers of Royal Marine courts martial are by division, with separate volumes for expeditionary battalions formed for the Carlist and China Wars of the 1830s and 1850s. Twentieth-century records are not all open yet (see Chapter 4 for detailed references for all these). ADM 12/21–26 contains legal analyses of naval courts martial 1755–1806 by offence, while the *Gentleman's Magazine* and *Naval Chronicle* feature courts martial and executions in more lurid detail.

2.4 Uniform and equipment

The material attributes of a soldier set him apart both from those pursuing other trades and members of other regiments or corps. Variations in dress, insignia and armament can reveal the date or place of a photograph, or identify the unit affiliation of the owner of a cap badge. Military uniforms and equipment are a subject in themselves, to which a book aimed at family historians can provide only the briefest overview. Those wishing to know more should consult James Ladd (*By Sea, By Land,* Appendix 3) for developments since 1919, or Stadden and Newark (*Uniforms of the Royal Marines*) for the longer view. The Royal Marine Museum holds the official dress regulations (BR81), and in-service training guides describing specialist Arctic and other equipment.

2.4.1 Clothing

Marine uniforms resemble those of line infantry, with some exceptions. The most striking anomalies are the tawny yellow worn by the Admiral's Regiment, and today's dark blue full dress. The former is sometimes explained as peculiar to the Duke of York, and sometimes as an echo of the New Model Army. It had disappeared by 1688. Dark blue is inherited from the RMA, who dressed as artillery rather than infantry for reasons discussed in section 1.2.3.

The best way to understand the evolution of marine uniform is not to read about it. It is better to study illustrations, such as the series of groups of marines from 1664 to 1973 painted by Stadden, which appears in the RMHS's *Short History* (pages 34–7). These have the advantage of presenting a large number of figures together for easy comparison, from which key points emerge:

- Coats become shorter and less full during the eighteenth century, the skirts turned back in the 1740s, culminating in the waist-length jacket or coatee of the Napoleonic period. Skirted tunics replace the jacket after the Crimean War, and still predominate, despite the 1940s blouson style battledress.

- Cuffs, lapels and collars become less pronounced. Stiff stand-up collars and leather stocks (hence 'bootneck') replace civilian style turned down collars towards 1800. Lapels button across to create the coatee, concealing the waistcoat. Originally in various colours depending on the regiment, collars and lapels become white in 1755, and blue when the Corps became Royal. The RMA's red facings with a blue coat reverse the usual pattern.
- Knee breeches with stockings or

Royal Marines collar badge: worn on the tunic collar, this badge can help identify a photograph when the subject is bareheaded.

'spatterdashes' make way for looser 'overall' trousers after the Napoleonic Wars, although shorter gaiters reappear periodically in service dress.

- Various patterns of belts and cross straps are worn at different times, and by different ranks, for example, the red shoulder sashes of senior NCOs, or the Sam Browne belts of twentieth-century officers. White pipeclay replaces buff leather, making way for drab coloured webbing after the Boer War (1899–1902).
- Musicians wear especially elaborate uniforms with gold braid or lace on sleeves and down the back, 'frogging' across the chest, and extravagantly decorated belts for drum majors.

Marines usually had a working dress as well as the full dress worn on parade. At sea they were often indistinguishable from the sailors. Marine officers were advised not to rig in red, but to lock up their detachment's uniforms, to keep them away from salt water and pitch. The marines on HMS *Victory*'s gun decks wore check shirts and dark blue trousers, not the red jackets seen in so many paintings. Around Chatham Barracks in the 1780s marines wore 'trowzers' and 'a close jacket' cut down from old uniform coats, the new ones only appearing on guard duty. Simplified undress uniforms were worn in the nineteenth century and early twentieth centuries, while at sea marines wore coarse white duck which could be boiled clean after coaling ship.

Service dress originated in North America. Marines who landed at Louisburg in 1746 wore cropped hats, short jackets and a blanket roll. At Bunker Hill they left coats and packs at the bottom, attacking in shirt sleeves. Local modifications became more common during the nineteenth century. RMLI serving with naval brigades wore red tunics and duck trousers, and stained white helmets with coffee. White drill tunics were made uniform in hot climates from 1875. In Egypt in 1882 the RMLI fought in blue, becoming known as 'the Blue Devils'. In the Sudan the Camel Corps wore grey. Khaki, meaning 'dust' in Hindustani, became standard from the Boer War, evolving through the field service and battledress of two world wars into today's Soldier 95 Combats.

2.4.2 Headdress

No item of dress is more distinctive than a hat, or more suggestive of a period. Early military headgear followed civilian styles, evolving into a bewildering variety of fur caps, shakos, helmets and berets. As usual, marines followed the general trend, adding their own characteristic variations.

Early eighteenth-century marines wore 'sugarloaf' mitre caps, like the line infantry's grenadier caps, but lower. If early uniforms bear any practical explanation, these allowed marines to sling their muskets more readily than

Studio photograph of Private William Walter Brockwell RMLI, taken at Deal in 1886. He is wearing the glengarry cap, with the full dress home service helmet visible on the left.

Royal Marine Artillery cap badge: a brass badge used by the RMA in various designs from 1860 to 1923, confusingly similar to badges used by the Royal Artillery and some army regiments.

the broad brimmed hat. By the 1770s, however, the three-cornered hat was standard, 'well cocked not flapped', with fur caps only for grenadiers. When line infantry adopted cylindrical shakos about 1800, marines went into their unique round hat with its narrow brim well laced up, as worn at Trafalgar. After the Napoleonic Wars the Corps adopted more military styles, bell topped shakos followed by the narrower 'Albert pot'.

The RMLI took the new lower shako introduced after the Crimean War, while the RMA went their own way with a cylindrical fur busby. Both adopted helmets in the late 1870s: white topees in tropical climates, often with a puggaree wrapped around, or blue spiked helmets like the Prussian pickelhaube at home. A white 'universal pattern' helmet was introduced in 1905, remaining the Royal Marines' ceremonial headdress to this day.

Marines always had working caps at sea, though their form is obscure. Pillbox shaped forage hats appeared in the nineteenth century, sometimes with a patent leather peak, and in tropical climates a white cloth cover and neck flap, or 'havelock'. The RMA kept their pillboxes when the RMLI adopted the glengarry in 1870, followed by fore-and-aft field service caps in 1897. The Brodrick (*sic*) replaced both in 1902, a round flat cap with no peak, so ugly it was said only the marines would have it. Officers and bandsmen, who wore round peaked caps as today, escaped this horror. It lasted, sometimes with a white cover, until the 1930s. Blue and khaki field service caps were worn at sea or ashore respectively, until the

Royal Marines other ranks helmet plate, as worn on the full dress helmet, and developed from the nineteenth-century shako plate.

introduction of blue berets for marines other than commandos in 1943. The latter wore green berets from formation, as do practically all members of the Corps today, except bandsmen and recruits in training. Steel helmets have been worn in action ashore since 1916.

2.4.3 Buttons and badges

The most common material evidence of an ancestor's service is likely to be his cap and collar badges, or tunic buttons. Military insignia has three main purposes: to distinguish one corps from another; to show rank; and to identify soldiers possessing special attributes. As with uniforms, badges are a study in themselves. Readers wishing to know more should consult James Ladd (*By Sea, By Land*, Appendix 3), or May, Carman and Tanner (*Badges and Insignia of the British Armed Services*).

The earliest known marine badge is the Garter Star on the front flap of the 'sugarloaf' caps of the 1740s. The Admiralty's foul anchor also came into use about then, appearing on buttons recovered from the 1758 wreck of the *Invincible* and on metal shoulder badges used until the Crimean War. The

Royal Marine officers 'staybright' cap badge (1953–present). Officers' badges may be identified by the separation of the lion and crown from the globe and laurel.

Other ranks RMLI cap badge (1855–1923). The bugle horn was a common device for light infantry and was also used by army regiments.

badge most commonly associated with the Corps is the great Globe surrounded by the laurel wreath, awarded by George IV in 1827. Unable to choose between over 100 battle honours submitted for royal approval, he directed the Royal Marines should wear the Globe and Laurel in recognition of their worldwide service. This is often combined with other symbols, for instance on the green beret with a lion and crown, disrespectfully known as the 'dog and basket'. The RMA were distinguished by the Royal Artillery's flaming grenade, the RMLI adopting the light infantry bugle horn in 1855. Both these devices disappeared on amalgamation in 1923.

The Second World War produced two new arm badges:

- Combined Operations Organization's circular or tombstone shaped cloth badge featuring an eagle, tommy gun, and kedge anchor, known to some as the 'Crapping Seagull Badge' (see front cover).
- The red commando fighting knife on a blue cloth sleeve patch.

Eighteenth-century marine NCOs wore shoulder-knots, before adopting the familiar chevrons in 1807. These were originally on both sleeves, on the right arm only from 1857. These should not be confused with GCBs, worn point upwards on the lower sleeve, initially on the right, then on the left from 1881.

Colour sergeants wore complex badges combining the crown, Globe and Laurel, union flag, and crossed swords or gun barrels, with one or three gold chevrons. Quartermaster-sergeant instructors wore a large crown on the right sleeve with an indication of their speciality: nothing extra for

365TH KING'S SQUAD

PASSED FOR DUTY 23RD MARCH, 1940

Osborne Hindmarsh Cooper Whitehead Kirkland Trendall McLaughlin Norman Pike Crouch Palmer Ilsley

S.Lock Dear Eastgate Leyster Cradock Kewley Nash Moyle Chapman Johnstone Powell H.Lock

Anderson (s.c.) Harding (s.c.) Tuffey (s.c.) Richmond (s.c.) Frost (s.c.) Webster North (s.c.) Hayward (s.c.) Drury (s.c.) Holznott (s.c.) Felton

Shuttlewood Q.M.S.I. A. Bell Capt. J. P. Phillips Jacob Sgt-Major L. B. Band Sgt. E. Fishlock
Q.M.S.I. Infantry. *Adjutant.* *Sgt-Major. Parade.* *Instructor.*

Group photograph of 365th King's Squad. The best squad of recruits in every batch to pass training were known as the King's Squad. These photographs are usually captioned with names.

infantry, crossed gun barrels for gunnery, muskets for musketry, Indian clubs for physical training. Letters identify more recent specialists, for example, 'AE' for assault engineers, or 'LC' for landing craft. One distinction unique to the Corps is the King's Badge awarded to the best recruit of the senior squad, known as the King's Squad. This bears the royal cipher of George V, who inaugurated the award after inspecting the Depot in 1918. The recipient wears it throughout his service, regardless of rank.

The different elements of the band service (see section 1.4) had and, to some extent, still do have their own distinctive badges. Buglers wore the Globe and Laurel, as did divisional bandsmen with various honorary badges. For example, the Prince of Wales's feathers worn by the Portsmouth and Plymouth RMLI bands commemorated royal tours with the future Edward VII and Edward VIII respectively. Band service musicians were distinguished by the lyre cap and collar badge, and the letters 'RMB' on their shoulder straps, until their replacement in 1946 by the general service 'RM'. Another musical distinction was the broad trouser stripe peculiar to divisional bands until amalgamation in 1950, when it became standard across the band service. Buglers, however, still wear the thin stripe.

2.4.4 Personal weapons

The marine's personal weapons altered little in appearance during the first half of his existence, reflecting limited technological change between the 1660s and 1840s. The 1850s ushered in a period of change which is still with us.

The marine has always been armed much as other infantrymen, with typical exceptions. The Admiral's had flintlock muskets throughout, rather than the mixture of pikes and matchlocks used by other Restoration regiments. For a sea soldier, the flintlock was safer and more reliable than a matchlock. The Duke's reverted to the conventional mixed armament, but William and Mary's marine regiments all carried flintlocks. These were smooth-bore single shot weapons loaded from the muzzle, posing little threat to anyone more than 100 yards away. The basic design hardly changed for over a century, beyond addition of a socket bayonet in the 1690s. Officers and sergeants carried pole-arms known as partisans, halberds or spontoons. Both frequently used muskets instead.

The mid-nineteenth century brought revolutionary changes in firearms. These changed their appearance as well as their effectiveness, making them a useful way of dating illustrations. The first improvement was a percussion lock fitted to smooth-bore muskets in 1842. This worked in the rain, and is recognizable from its characteristic nipple and flat hammer. Royal Marines had some with rifling, a spiral groove inside the barrel that spins the bullet, improving accuracy. Marines used both versions of the percussion musket in the Crimea as well as the army's 1851 pattern rifle known as the *Minié* from its French designer. All three were replaced by the Enfield rifle, a much better .577 calibre weapon used during the Indian Mutiny. Royal Marines had the full-length version with a straight triangular bayonet, as opposed to the short naval rifle used by seamen. The Enfield multiplied ranges by five, and dramatically improved accuracy. Rifles can be distinguished from smooth-bore weapons by flap sights above the barrel.

Rifles made it dangerous to stand up and reload under fire. In 1867 the British fitted Snider rolling block breech mechanisms to their Enfield rifles, allowing users to reload lying down, while doubling rates of fire. Marines used these against the Ashanti in 1874, not long before receiving a brand new rifle, the .45 Martini Henry. This had a falling breech, worked from below by a lever behind the trigger guard, giving the weapon a unique appearance, as seen in army hands in the film *Zulu*. The Martini Henry was shorter than its predecessors, 4ft 1½ins against 4ft 7ins, and had a wavy sword bayonet. It was an excellent rifle, used in Zululand, Egypt, the Sudan and Burma.

All these were large calibre rifles using black powder propellant. The next step was a small calibre magazine rifle using cordite, a smokeless propellant. This gave much higher muzzle velocities, a flat trajectory and a deeper danger space for the target. Marines received the .303 Lee Metford magazine rifle in 1895, using it during the 1897 Benin Expedition. The Lee Metford evolved into the Lee Enfield, used in the Boer War and both world wars in long and short versions. The Short Magazine Lee Enfield or SMLE continued in use until the 1960s. These all look very similar, with a bolt action and magazine beneath the stock, in front of the trigger guard. Shooting became a central feature of service life, its importance reflected in the extra pay earned by a first class shot or marksman. Competitions were often photographed and results published in *Globe & Laurel*.

The SMLE's replacement was the Belgian SLR or self-loading rifle, firing the NATO 7.62mm calibre round. This was used in Aden, Northern Ireland and in the Falklands, although units in Borneo and some specialists had the American Armalite automatic rifle. The SLR's distinguishing features include a pistol grip and large 20 round magazine. Since 1986 the Corps has used the SA80, a lighter automatic rifle with a short stock designed for easy handling in cramped spaces. Firing a 5.56mm round, it has experienced severe operability problems. Nevertheless the SA80 has served in the Gulf, Northern Ireland, Bosnia, Iraq and Afghanistan. It remains the standard British military rifle, and can be recognized by the large night sight on top, and the curved magazine behind the pistol grip.

2.5 Barrack life

Much of the tone of the Royal Marines derived from their being the first complete British corps to possess fixed headquarters. Barracks constructed at Portsmouth, Chatham and Plymouth between 1769 and 1783 provided institutional stability, which made up for the dispersal and unpredictability of sea service.

A succession of progressive commandants stamped their love of order upon the Corps, benefiting both the service and the individual marine. Printed instructions on barrack room walls reminded men of their duty, implying most could read. Order books regulated every aspect of barrack life: pewter chamber pots 'to prevent a nuisance in the Barracks', window cleaning, unauthorized going over the walls, sentries who defaced sentry boxes. Barrack women washed clothes and scoured bedsteads with hot water, soap and sand. Hygiene was as necessary in barracks as onboard ship:

> Particular care to be taken, that on no pretence whatsoever, are any old Cloathes, Rags, Living or Dead Dogs or Cats, or any other Animal or thing whatsoever, thrown into the Boghouses, which may prevent the Drains in performing their so necessary office.

Poaching and raiding orchards were banned, and sexual licence repressed. Officers doing the nightly rounds were instructed 'to enquire that no other women lye in the Men's Rooms, except those who are publickly appointed to that Business'. Health care was provided in case such precautions failed, infirmary expenses defrayed by stopping the pay of venereal patients: 10s for a sergeant, 6s for drummers and corporals, 5s for private men. Men slept two to a bed, but had lockers for their gear and mess tables to eat from, facilities many civilians lacked. Nineteenth-century barrack life contrasts favourably with Dickensian views of Victorian living conditions. Woolwich Barracks had a kitchen for every forty men and a Turkish bath. Chatham's drill shed became a roller-skating rink outside working hours. Eastney had a skittle alley and recreation room, which lent books and served tea or coffee.

Marines became family men, encouraged to marry by settled stations, short tours of duty overseas, and opportunities for paid work as boats' crew, carpenters, gardeners, grass cutters, lamplighters, painters, printers and storemen. RMA tradesmen repaired Eastney barracks, built a church and theatre, and made their own boots and clothes, a tradition of self-sufficiency that lasted into the twentieth century. Working hours were from 6 am to 6 pm in summer with an hour for breakfast and ninety minutes for lunch, starting two hours later in winter with an hour for lunch.

RMA gunners in their barrack room, Eastney Barracks, c. 1908.

Just inside the gate, a group of Edwardian RMA relax after church parade in the Brodrick cap and canvas gaiters peculiar to Royal Marines at that period.

Prospective husbands applied for permission to marry, the numbers allowed being limited. Their fiancées required references showing them fit persons to enjoy the advantages of becoming 'a married woman of the Royal Marines'. Once wed they found paid work as laundrywomen or seamstresses, making shirts for the Corps. Some lived in married quarters, where standing orders banned dogs, smoking or spitting in the corridors, and cleaning boots in the lavatories. Passages were swept twice daily, and dirty water emptied into sinks at the end of the block, except for bedroom slops which went into outdoor latrines. Children over four years slept in dormitories, put to bed by their parents, and attended school within the barracks. On Sundays they paraded with their schoolmaster or mistress, and marched to church. Other families rented accommodation outside barracks in places like Eastney's Adair Road or Kassassin Street, named respectively after a dynasty of Royal Marine officers and a Corps exploit in Egypt in 1882.

The closure of the Grand Divisions ended a way of life as well as a military system. Postwar marines have been too busy for spare-time jobs, while their wives would resent restrictions that once looked like advantages. Today they live on MoD estates around Norton Manor (40 Cdo), Bickleigh (42 Cdo), Arbroath (45 Cdo), and Lympstone (Training Centre). Domestic barrack life has left traces in spasmodic divisional registers of marriages, and births and deaths of children. Woolwich and the RMA registered baptisms instead of births. A centralized record of Royal Marine schools and teachers survives for 1840–90. National census returns for the barracks and surrounding streets may show a man's family, even when he himself was at sea.

2.6 Training

Cheeseparing Hanoverian politicians, and some naval historians, have denied that marines needed training – any yokel could be sent straight to sea from the plough's tail. There is more to a marine than sea-legs, however. As an opposition peer noted in 1739, 'they have more duties to learn and more difficulties to encounter' than land soldiers. They needed more training, not less. This has varied over time, but its aim has been constant. As the Commandant General wrote in 1946, 'The object of all training in the Royal Marines is to prepare the Corps to fight.'

Marine training suffers unusual constraints. Dispersal at sea and lack of space aboard ship present obvious difficulties. Some naval officers resented any soldiering in their ship, one compelling his detachment to exercise downwind from the galley chimney. First lieutenants had prior call on marines for work around the ship, with depressing consequences for morale and expertise. Naval captains who knew their business, however, exercised their detachments whenever the weather permitted, 'that they may not forget the Whole of what they have been taught on Shore'. Earl St Vincent put marine training before any ship duty, except getting under weigh. Disembarked marines returned to headquarters to be refreshed mentally as well as physically by two drills a day and twice weekly field days, a luxury denied eighteenth-century infantry regiments, who were scattered about the countryside preventing riots and smuggling.

Marine training resembles that of other infantrymen, with appropriate modifications. Hurried off to sea with raw detachments, eighteenth-century officers had little time for 'Complication of Manoeuvres, and Evolutions, which would be ridiculous in an Officer to attempt at sea'. They focused on the essential movements:

- Load and fire, with fixed bayonets
- Charge and halt
- Disperse and reform
- Recover arms, unfix bayonets, and dismiss.

When perfect, recruits practised loading and firing ball against a mark 'hung for the Purpose at the Extremity of the Fore-Yard Arm'. Early musketry

Group photograph of 24 Squad, Royal Marines 1940: produced after training was completed, these photographs can provide a date and identification even when there are no names.

Royal Marines musketry instructors at Malta in 1885. Note the frogging across the seated officer's tunic, and the NCOs' arm badges and sashes. The gold band and pillbox cap of the standing NCO shows he was RMA.

prioritized high rates of fire over accuracy. Well trained detachments might deliver four rounds a minute, compared with the two usual in a land fire-fight. Marksmanship training appears at Chatham in 1835, men being paid a shilling for hitting the bull's eye. By the 1860s marines competed for annual shooting badges, a regular feature of the modern infantryman's life.

Two hours' drill a day appears dull, but handling a heavy musket was good exercise when formal physical training did not exist. Sham fights across the deck were another substitute, best conducted without bayonets. The strangest gap in early marine training, and the most tragic, was the rank and file's ignorance of swimming. Only four of *Queen Charlotte*'s detachment escaped when she caught fire in harbour in 1800. Later marines swam from spars extended from their ship's side, but others were still non-swimmers. Many of HMS *Victoria*'s detachment drowned when she was accidentally sunk in 1893, prompting construction of swimming baths at Walmer and the three divisions.

Physical training in the modern sense was a nineteenth-century invention. Nathaniel Hiscock was run off his feet at Deal, with voluntary gym in the evening: 'muscles were trained . . . until we felt like elastic'. RND route marches left older men staggering like 'vessels in a rough sea'. Brains were not neglected. Late Victorian recruits attended school on alternate afternoons, until able to read and write 'fairly'. NCOs needed a good hand and a capacity for vulgar and decimal fractions. Corporals required a Third Class School Certificate, sergeants a First or Second.

71

Marine officers were not always as professional as they might have been. Lieutenant Tatton Brown wrote that one captain he knew was of 'no education', while another 'likes to see his men in good order yett does not know how to do it'. He himself went to sea after five months' training at headquarters. Graduates of the RMA's three and a half year training programme in the 1880s, however, could claim a better education than any combatant naval officer. Marine officers studied gunnery at HMS *Excellent*, musketry at Hythe and gymnastics and signalling at Aldershot, making them some of the most scientific officers in the service.

Two training areas unique to marines were naval gunnery and amphibious operations. The former was the passing product of circumstance; the latter now occupies what appears to be its logical place. Gunnery was not a function of early marines. They first appear at the great guns in the 1790s, usually in the higher numbered and less skilled posts. The RMA, however, gave marines better training in gunnery than their naval shipmates, who were paid off after every commission, losing whatever gunnery skills they had acquired. Artillery companies studied their business ashore, rigging a practice battery on Southsea Common like a ship's gun deck. In 1859 Fort Cumberland featured a 64pdr smooth-bore gun on trucks, mortars on turntables like those in bomb vessels, and a 6pdr battery on a rolling platform to simulate the motion of a ship. Facilities kept pace with modern developments, a 12in turret and director replacing older weapons by 1913. Marines knew every part of each gun, its function and how to strip it down. If a class became slack, there was extra drill, humping 100lb shells into the dummy loader, leaving strong men like limp rags. Practice made perfect. One of HMS *Exeter*'s detachment remembered the Battle of the Java Sea in 1942 as a prolonged gunnery drill, with no idea of losing until her lights went out. The disappearance of the big gun from naval armaments after the Second World War ended the Royal Marines' gunnery role, and the training that went with it.

Marines took part in numerous amphibious operations during the first decade of the eighteenth century. Training was on the job, consisting of the boat work that formed part of every ship's routine. The preparations were simply those required to keep arms and ammunition dry. Little more was needed while effective small arms range was under 100 yards. Once a body of infantry was ashore the usual land tactics applied. Landing operations as practised by nineteenth-century squadrons focused less on getting ashore than what was done next – a marine colonel at Gallipoli in 1915 finding regular infantry more adept at boat work than his own men. Interwar attitudes remained ambivalent. Officer classes at Deal never witnessed the landing of a platoon from a cutter on an open beach, although the recruits practised the operation.

All this changed in 1943. Some Royal Marines went to Achnacarry near Fort

William for the commando course; others to Largs in the Firth of Clyde and Inverary on Loch Fyne to become landing craft crew. Lance corporal coxswains studied combined operations doctrine, equipment and drills, their notebooks reminiscent of those created by student gunnery officers in the 1840s. One wrote hopefully, 'Disasterous (*sic*) results of old time landings have now been rectified'. Training, amphibious and otherwise, became the mantra of the Corps. Arctic exercises became so routine in the 1970s that Royal Marine helicopter pilots could say if it was January, it must be Norway.

The content of marine training may matter less to family historians than its location. Formal training was at divisional headquarters until 1861, when Deal became the recruit training depot, away from the temptations of the home ports. 'Beware of the ladies,' said Private Hiscock's drill sergeant, 'we have none here.' Drop out rates were high – thirty of his squad of seventy. Recruits went to their divisions for field training and gunnery after eight months at Deal. The RMA used Fort Cumberland, known as the Repository, for gunnery and experimental work, MNBDO taking over during the Second World War, and afterwards the Technical Training Depot. The RND took men from Deal for further training at Blandford Camp, and then at its own Infantry Base Depot near Calais, distinct from the army's bullring at Étaples. Walter Popham remembered Blandford as 'wild and bleak', the water taps frozen solid and physical training 'a hardening of horror'.

Twentieth-century weapons needed more space, prompting moves to new establishments. The Corps has occupied various sites near Lympstone in Devon since the 1940s, first at Exton Camp, and then across the road in what has since become Commando Training Centre RM (CTCRM). In 1943 Lympstone replaced Deal as *the* Depot. Infantry Training was also conducted at Dalditch Camp until 1946, and then at Bickleigh near Plymouth, until the Commando School moved to Lympstone in 1960.

A Small Arms School established at Browndown near Gosport in 1916 outgrew the ranges in the 1950s, moving to Lympstone. Class photographs at the Royal Marines Museum provide an unusually certain way of identifying students. More transient establishments were the RM Officer Cadet Training Unit (OCTU) at Thurlestone in Devon, which existed between January 1941 and August 1946, and several camps in North Wales around Tywyn and Barmouth. This is not an exhaustive list of RM establishments, for which readers should see James Ladd (*By Sea, By Land*, pages 544–9).

2.7 Going to sea

The objective of everything discussed in this chapter, for most of the history of the Corps, was to supply detachments of marines for ships of the Royal

An informal group photograph, made into a postcard, of marines and seamen in the cruiser HMS Achilles, 1915. The Royal Marines are clearly identifiable by their headdress and badges, and more military dress.

Navy. The first recorded instance of this was the embarkation of two companies of the Admiral's Regiment in May 1665 in the *Loyall Subject* and *Baltimore*. For nearly 300 years sea service was the ultimate fulfilment of all the effort expended on raising, feeding, clothing and training marines.

The conditions they faced are hard to envisage today. Life aboard a Stuart or Georgian warship must have been a shock to landsmen. Colonel Edye wondered how, 'In view . . . of the utter want of organization and comfort that then prevailed afloat . . . discipline was maintained and contentment secured.' A freshly embarked subaltern of the 1780s was appalled by the 'unguided tumult and undisciplined confusion', which, 'involved all arrangements in one universal chaos'. Another officer described his berth as, 'a place between two guns, about seven foot long and four feet wide, and divided only from some hundred hammocks by a little canvas or an old sail, where there is no light but for a candle, nor no air but what is unavoidably very foul'. Another thought he was housed worse than a dog. Conditions for other ranks, fed and berthed as the seamen, were no better.

Marines at sea came under naval authority from earliest times. Exercised without tact, this necessary subordination caused considerable friction. A veteran of the 1740s complained that 'A captain of marines, though of the highest quality, may be confined by the cook of the ship [then a warrant officer], the lowest of their Officers having the command on board over the highest of ours.' The Admiralty had to insist on marine officers being treated as gentlemen, 'with the decency and regard due to the Commissions they bear'. Other ranks worked the same 'relieves and tours of duty' as the seamen, forming two watches at sea, and three in harbour. Their places in muster bills reflect their lack of nautical skills, alongside less active seamen as 'waisters', or on the quarterdeck. They assisted with labour-intensive tasks such as pumping ship or unmooring, taking their turn at the capstan. Subject to naval officers while performing nautical tasks, they were 'not to be obliged to go aloft, or be beat or punished for not showing any inclination to do so'. Such injunctions might mean little. A satirical pamphlet of the 1770s recommended sea officers kept a good oak stick to avoid breaking their speaking trumpet on the marines.

Improved ship design and social manners ameliorated the lot of the Victorian marine. Steam engines heated washing machines, as in HMS *Warrior*, and reduced donkey work. Long service marines knew as much about seamanship as sailors trained in barracks. Living conditions remained spartan, but mess decks were orderly and clean compared with the Georgian navy. While waiting for the Germans, First World War marines amused themselves with cinema shows, mandolins, and wind-up gramophones. One physical task nobody could escape was coaling ship, a filthy, back-breaking

Marine detachment on parade on the quarter deck of the cruiser HMS Impérieuse in the 1890s, showing the lack of space for military work afloat.

task that filled every corner of the ship, including the eyes, ears, mouths and noses of the crew, with coal dust. Coaling had to be done quickly, as a ship with empty bunkers presented a sitting target. The battle cruiser *Princess Royal* took in 2,260 tons in fifteen hours at Jamaica in 1914, with three twenty-minute breaks.

The Admiral's Regiment had rarely served long at sea, while few cruises in the 1690s lasted many weeks. This changed as British fleets moved into the Mediterranean. A company of Churchill's Marines received 462 days continuous sea pay in 1706, a figure soon exceeded as Britain fought world wars in India and America. The detachment of HMS *Defiance* petitioned for relief in 1798 after five years away from headquarters, having been turned over at sea from another ship, contrary to the spirit of *Admiralty Instructions*. An officer expected to serve two, three or more years successively, after which he was not to be re-embarked 'till all the Officers of his Rank on Shore, of the Division to which he belongs shall have served an equal Time with him at Sea'. Steam brought shorter commissions, but even steamships might be away for two or three years on remote stations. The reduced strength of the Corps in proportion to the Royal Navy during the 1920s brought complaints that the burden of sea service was unequally shared, with deleterious consequences for morale and training.

The size of a detachment depended on the class of warship, and varied over time. An average strength in 1668 was twelve, just enough for the captain's guard. Later detachments were considerably larger. In 1704 HMS *Falmouth* (58 guns) had a complement of 257, including 47 marines and one woman. Regulations of 1747 allowed roughly one private marine per heavy gun. Numbers ranged from 100 private marines for a 1st rate ship of the line like *Victory*, to 50 in a 5th rate frigate, and 20 in a sloop. Officers and NCOs were in proportion, captains serving only in 4th rates (50–60 guns) and above. Detachments in larger warships crept up, exceeding 160 in a 1st rate towards the end of the sailing navy. HMS *Warrior*, the first all iron battleship, had 114 Gunners RMA as well as 11 officers, NCOs, and drummers. Numbers peaked again between the world wars: HMS *Nelson* had 150 marines in 1939, besides 53 officers, NCOs and musicians. Cruisers were more modest: HMS *Ajax*, engaged at the River Plate in 1939, had 46 and 24. Sea service dwindled with the passing of battleships and big gun cruisers. Postwar detachments returned to seventeenth-century proportions, with just ten marines in *Leander*-class frigates. Ships finally stopped embarking detachments in 1998, a Fleet Standby Rifle Troop providing six-man teams to support anti-terrorist and anti-piracy operations as needed.

The flow of manpower was regulated by the sea service roster maintained at each headquarters. Officers were to take their 'Tour of Duty at Sea' in strict rotation, those next for sea to remain in readiness at headquarters. Anyone who missed their turn, through ill health or other reason, moved straight to the top of the list on their return. The process was less orderly in practice. Cheated of a potentially lucrative place in a frigate in 1806 Lewis Roteley threatened to write to the Admiralty 'and make it known to them how irregular the Roaster [sic] is kept with respect to their Embarking Officers out of their turn'.

Regulations discouraged the practice of turning marines over from one ship to another, which might throw the whole process into confusion. Naval officers commanding ports where ships needed marines had to apply in due form to headquarters, returning unsatisfactory men with 'reasons in writing under his hand for such a refusal'. The discharge of marines to shore, or from one ship to another, will appear in the ship's muster books, when these exist, and may feature in the ship's log. These rarely mention names, but do outline the ship's movements and activities. The names of her officers also appear in the *Navy List*, making it possible to track RM Officers joining or leaving particular vessels.

Eighteenth-century divisional orders are laconic, specifying so many marines to embark in a specified ship, but naming only the officers. Few divisional embarkation books survive at the National Archives, and others may be too fragile to produce. Drafting policy was benign, pitching first upon 'such men as have the shortest time at sea, and such as may be in debt to the Crown'. Adjutants and quartermasters were to ensure that those selected were 'forwardest in their Discipline, and Military Knowledge', and, 'furnished with proper Arms and Accoutrements and every other thing necessary'. Departures became less arbitrary in the nineteenth century, the 'Top Hundred for Sea' listed on orderly room notice boards. The system reached a peak of sophistication in the 1940s, the drafting office combing separate card files for different ranks and specialities to allocate places at sea to those with least recent sea time. Wall and Ritson explain its operation in *The Royal Marine Pocket Book* (pages 56–8).

Shipboard conditions threatened both health and equipment of marine detachments. Charles II had recognized the difficulties of keeping weapons in working order at sea in 1670, when ordering fresh pikes, firelocks and 'collars of bandoleers' for the Admiral's Regiment. The Admiralty addressed the problem in the 1740s, issuing instructions 'for Chests to be made to contain the Arms and Ammunition of the Marines serving on board each man of war, and a storeroom to be built on the Orlop to contain the spare Cloathing, accoutrements, etc'. As marines came aboard the wise officer relieved them of their new hats, coats and white shirts, to keep them clean. Muskets and ammunition went into separate arms chests lashed onto the grating abaft the mizzenmast, near the marines' action station on the quarterdeck. OCRMs kept their store cupboard to the end of sea service, Bren guns and projectors, infantry, anti-tank co-habiting with more traditional material.

Early sea kit was sparse: bed, blanket and pillow; two speckled shirts and cravats; two pairs of shoes and hose; 2lb of tobacco; a knapsack; spatter-dashes; plus a frying pan, kettle, and chest to every six men. Few eighteenth-century marines had anything beyond their clothes, perhaps a snuff box or a pen knife. Necessities supplied from their pay included pipe clay, soap, thread and needles. Victorian marines were better provided, with greatcoats, mess tins, and clothes brushes, as well as such oddities as button sticks and knee-caps. Official and unofficial sea kit continued to expand, reflecting increased prosperity, and perhaps bureaucratic realization that there is no point sending men to sea with insufficient clothing to keep them alive and healthy. See Wall and Ritson, pages 76–9, for kit issued towards the end of sea service in the 1940s.

Chapter 3

OPERATIONS – WHAT MARINES DO

The object of military forces is to fight. The Royal Marines and their predecessors have seen action in every area of the world, from Albania to
Zanzibar. This chapter gives an impression of the type of operations in which
they have been involved. The first two sections cover the distinct naval or military operations typical of the Corps before 1943, the third the amphibious
operations that have since become its bread and butter. The chapter concludes
by considering the human cost, and how a marine's career might end.

3.1 At sea

A ship's marine detachment had two combat roles. It contributed to sea
actions alongside other members of her complement, and took the lead in any
landing force she might send ashore. When not under fire, marines performed
routine military tasks, enhancing the security and dignity of life at sea.

3.1.1 Naval actions

The Royal Marines' experience of naval combat began with the Dutch Wars
of the 1660s. It continued through the long eighteenth-century struggle against
France and Spain, and ended with the defeat of Germany in two world wars.
That experience falls into two very distinct categories: action under sail, and
action under steam.

Naval battles under sail were characterized by short ranges and limited
mobility. Ships moved only as the wind allowed. The masts and sails on which
their movement depended were usually among the first casualties. Armament
consisted of smooth-bore guns distributed along either broadside, firing at
right angles to the direction of movement. A ship might easily be immobilized,
with an enemy ship across one end subjecting her to raking fire, to which her
main armament could not reply. Marines, who could move swiftly to the

Early marines in characteristic sugarloaf caps, manning their action stations on the poop deck of an eighteenth-century warship. (Cyril Field)

The battlecruiser HMS Lion after the Battle of Jutland in 1916, a typical example of the capital ships of her day. The roof of 'Q' turret, between the funnels, has been ripped open by a direct hit, killing most of the fifty marines inside and below.

threatened point, were essential in such emergencies. Contrary to popular belief, they rarely took to the rigging as snipers. Marines wore shoes and were not expected to go aloft. Their post was on the poop or forecastle, covering the ship's vulnerable ends. Neither did they lead boarding parties. That was better done by barefoot seamen with cutlasses. The marines' forte was clearing enemy decks with concentrated blasts of musketry, their bayonets an ultimate deterrent against hostile boarders.

Lewis Rotely left this account of *Victory's* gun decks at Trafalgar:

> a battle in a three decker . . . beggars all description it bewilders the senses of sight and hearing, there was the fire from above, the fire from below besides the fire from the deck I was upon… reports louder than thunder the decks heaving. I fancied myself in the infernal regions where every man appeared a devil. Lips might move but orders and hearing were out of the question.

Steamships could manoeuvre as they wished. Engines below the waterline were safe from all but the most unlucky hit. Guns acquired rifling, and grew to a monstrous size. The 13.5in gun mounted in British 'super-dreadnoughts' during the First World War weighed 76 tons, and fired a 1,400lb shell to 23,200yds. Battles were at extreme visible range, gun flashes on the horizon the only sign of the enemy. Redundant as small arms parties, Royal Marines fought behind armour, in one of their ship's main turrets and its associated ammunition handing room and magazine. Usually they were in 'X' or 'Q' turret, just abaft the funnels. Major Harvey in HMS *Lion* felt quite detached, 'fighting in a turret one doesn't suffer discomfort and my chief feeling has been that of "curiosity" mixed with the idea that whoever else is coming to grief, oneself will be alright!'. Death either took nobody or whole detachments. When HMS *Invincible* blew up at Jutland, only one of her 106 marines survived.

Bandsmen shared the Corps' gunnery role, manning the nerve centre of the ship's fire control system in the transmitting station (T/S). In action they processed data passed to them from the director, high up in the ship, to calculate ranges and bearings of targets for their shipmates at the guns. Deep below the waterline, surrounded by fuel and ammunition, the T/S was a death trap. RM bandsmen of the Second World War lost a quarter of their strength killed, a higher percentage than any other service.

Submarines and aircraft changed the marines' gunnery role. Pensioners and reservists were recalled to serve in defensively equipped merchant ships or DEMS, training merchant seamen on all sorts of unlikely guns, from 4.7in quick-firers to bomb throwers made from drainpipe. Ships' detachments manned anti-aircraft guns mounted on the main turrets of battleships, or covered Second World War evacuations from converted anti-aircraft cruisers. Lieutenant Philip Beeman was sunk twice. He did not recall his first ship, HMS *Calcutta*, 'ever going to sea without suffering air attack of one kind or another'.

The Royal Navy's last traditional sea action was the sinking of the German battlecruiser *Scharnhorst* off Norway's North Cape on Boxing Day 1943. Numerous Royal Marines, however, took part in shore bombardments off Salerno and Normandy, and Korea in the early 1950s. The 6in cruiser HMS *Arethusa* lay off the Normandy beaches for nearly three weeks, dropping shells onto German tanks, while dodging glider bombs and parachute mines. Concussion from her own guns split the upper decks, asbestos trickling onto mess tables below, light bulbs flying whenever 'A' and 'B' turrets fired a full broadside. Eventually she hit two mines, while going astern to avoid another, smashing her fire control machinery, and jamming 'Y' turret.

Naval actions are heavily documented in primary and secondary sources. If a marine's ship is known, it is not difficult to establish the actions in which she participated from a standard naval history such as that of Clowes (see Further Reading). Alternatively, if a man served at a particular battle it is possible to search muster rolls for all ships taking part, to establish which one he was in. Individual actions are less easy to establish. Naval despatches rarely mention marine officers, let alone other ranks. Muster rolls show whether a man was onboard before or after an action, but give no clue as to what he did. Navy lists perform a similar function for officers in later actions. Casualty lists sometimes give names and severity of wounds, while monuments at the Royal Navy's three home ports commemorate marines lost at sea in both world wars in chronological order, following naval personnel.

3.1.2 Landing parties and naval brigades

Ships are never free of the shore. Operating on a hostile coast they need military forces to cover minor landings, to lead raids on harbours and coastal defences, or to form the core of more substantial expeditions. Ships' marine detachments enabled them to conduct littoral warfare, using only their own resources.

Before drinking water could be condensed from steam or food preserved in tins, warships constantly put ashore for fresh water and vegetables. Marine detachments played two roles in these domestic expeditions, protecting unarmed seamen against attack and stopping them deserting. Eighteenth-century marines developed considerable expertise in leaping ashore from ships' boats, dry cartridges in their hats, and forming up on the beach before the fleet had come to anchor. Such affairs were not risk free. Spanish cavalry

Ship's boats dash out from the side of HMS Surprise *in 1799: marines provided the military muscle for minor amphibious operations throughout the eighteenth and nineteenth centuries.*

killed two sailors stealing onions near Malaga in 1704 and nearly caught Admiral Dilkes fishing, but the marines covered the withdrawal without further loss. Thomas Wybourn described a more idyllic scene at Palma Bay in Sardinia in 1805, the guard pitching tents on a flower-covered riverbank, where they dined their friends, 'after the fashion of the Gipsies'. Sailors rolled water casks up and down the beach, while local people sold livestock, fresh fruit and vegetables, 'the whole shore . . . like a Camp and Fair united'. An officer's handbook from the 1840s still recommended posting sentries while washing hammocks ashore, 'to keep those who may be irregularly disposed, within the prescribed bounds'.

Skills developed in this trivial fashion bore serious fruit. Marines secured landing beaches for the army, as at Guadeloupe in 1759, and evacuations, as at Boston in 1776. Once the Royal Navy had swept Napoleon's fleets from the sea, marines raided harbours to cut out merchantmen, or stormed batteries protecting privateers. They were uniquely suited to such operations. Loading boats at night with soldiers unaccustomed to the sea, and disembarking them on a hostile shore, would have been impossibly difficult. Opposing Nelson's undrilled seamen to regular troops on land would have courted disaster. The

Naval Chronicle leaves no doubt about the combined effectiveness of marines and seamen, the one storming enemy positions at bayonet point, to cover the other's cutting out and demolition work. From 1812, the Mediterranean and Channel Fleets were assigned additional marines for use 'in destroying signal communications and other petty harassing modes of warfare'. British moral superiority was such that opponents frequently offered no resistance, preferring to spike their guns, and run away.

The Napoleonic Wars left Britain the dominant world power. For almost a century the Royal Navy acted as an international policeman. Home governments could easily disavow naval action, making Royal Marines ideal for intervening in trouble spots, winning such ironic titles as 'Lord Palmerston's Own' and 'The Old Tagus Rangers'. Many of these operations have a modern ring: hostage rescue at Algiers in 1816, or international efforts to prevent genocide in Greece, culminating in destruction of an Ottoman fleet at Navarino in 1827.

Lacking maritime opponents, thrusting naval officers put together ad hoc landing forces, known as naval brigades, and sought action ashore. A naval brigade could come from one or more ships, typically consisting of a company of marines, with two of bluejacket riflemen, besides naval field gun and machine-gun crews, demolition parties and stretcher-bearers. A large brigade might be 500 strong, a fifth or quarter of them marines. Some mounted heavy cannon on mobile field carriages and acted as siege trains, as they did at Sebastopol in 1854–5, and Lucknow during the Indian Mutiny of 1857. In that case marines escorted the guns, as they did again in 1899 during the Boer War. Other naval brigades acted as columns of all arms, sometimes alone, sometimes with the army.

Naval brigades served in China in the 1840s and 1850s, Burma, Egypt and the Sudan in the 1880s, as well the Maori, Ashanti and Zulu Wars (1860–4, 1873–4 and 1879). Africa was their great playground, forces landing to do a job and re-embarking before malaria set in. Naval brigades were particularly valuable during the 'Scramble for Africa' in the 1890s, with deployments at Witu, the Gambia, and Benin. Marines formed the backbone of such operations. When bluejackets were sent back to conserve supplies during the Benin campaign, all available marines were retained for the final push.

Naval brigades faded away with the nineteenth century. Their last major commitment was in China in 1900, during the conflict known in Britain as the Boxer Rebellion, remembered for the defence of the diplomatic legations at Peking. Previously backward opponents now had the latest modern weapons. Royal Marines lost 44 per cent of their strength (eleven killed, seventy-three wounded) in a frontal attack on Boer 'farmers' at Graspan in November 1899, an unsustainable loss rate. Meanwhile Germany had emerged as a new and dangerous rival at sea, compelling the Royal Navy to concentrate in home waters, returning to its traditional role of securing command of the sea.

Official and secondary accounts rarely focus on individual members of landing parties, although Laird Clowes's *The Royal Navy* and Richard Brooks's *Long Arm of Empire* cover naval brigades in considerable operational detail. Victorian interest in the empire and increasing literacy generated numerous first-hand accounts, many reprinted by Naval and Military press. Local papers covered the return of veterans, as did the *Illustrated London News*. Memorials in home ports often commemorate names of the dead, for example those in Portsmouth's Victoria Park dedicated to HMS *Active* (Zulu War) and *Centurion* (Boxer Rebellion).

3.1.3 Routine and ceremonial

Marines spent only a small proportion of their sea time in action. When no enemy was in sight, they secured their ship from other threats.

The most important military function of marines, when not in action, was as sentries. A 74-gun ship of Nelson's day posted fifteen sentinels, two each at quarterdeck, pump, gangway and forecastle; one each at the ward room, gun room, fore and after cockpit, galley, bits, and prisoners. Sentries in harbour wore full uniform and powdered hair (until 1806, later than the army), with full ammunition pouches and canteens. Sentries had twenty-four hours to clean up before mounting guard, and might not be called for other duties. At sea, they made the best appearance they could in their second clothing.

Sentries controlled access to the ship, ensuring no boats ran alongside without permission, or unauthorized persons and packages entered or left the ship, particularly women or people selling liquor. At night sentries on the upper decks called out 'All's Well' every quarter hour, raising the alarm if the word was not repeated around the ship. They were also meant to fire on anyone jumping overboard or into a boat, but this was risky. A marine who shot a deserter in 1759, at the instance of two naval warrant officers, was tried for murder at the Old Bailey, and all three branded for manslaughter.

A sentry's duties within a warship included preventing access to the officers' quarters, except by servants, controlling the issue of water from the scuttlebutt and stopping others from using the galley while the officers' dinners were cooked. He was not to allow rubbish to be thrown out of the ports, nor permit unnecessary noise and lights near his post. After dark marine NCOs patrolled the ship with the master-at-arms, putting out lights and fires. Marines also guarded prisoners of war, ensuring they remained quiet and sober. When moving prisoners by boat, it was best to tow them separately, marines in a third boat ready to open fire. Eighteenth-century seamen showed little respect for sentries, but Earl St Vincent, Commander-in-Chief in the

Ceremonial was an important feature of a Royal's existence: marines parade through Palace Square in Valletta, Malta, in 1908.

Mediterranean, changed this, ordering a seaman 100 lashes for knocking a sentry down.

One advantage for the naval authorities of employing two separate classes of men at sea was the possibility of setting one against the other. Marines were traditionally used to repress mutinous behaviour by the seamen. As early as the 1690s marine detachments kept their arms in the after part of the ship, away from the sailors. John Howe describes an armed stand-off between angry seamen and loyal marines in *Defiance* in 1779. The most dangerous naval mutinies were at Spithead and the Nore in 1797, when the Channel and North Sea fleets refused duty until pay and rations were improved. Early Corps historians claimed the marines remained loyal throughout, but reality was more complex. Those on shore did so. Thomas Wybourn's first active service was against the Nore mutineers. Marines at sea generally sided with their shipmates, whose grievances they shared.

Part of the official response to the mutinies was to differentiate marines more sharply from seamen. St Vincent implemented earlier proposals to berth marines between officers and ratings, and took steps to improve the marines' status, emphasizing their distinct military identity. He stressed formal discipline, enhanced the authority of marine officers and NCOs, enforced uniformity of dress among the fleet's detachments, and himself attended guard mounting every morning in full dress, while the band played 'God Save the King'. Marine bands and guards of honour remained an important part of naval ceremonial long after St Vincent's original reasoning had lost its force.

Ingrained discipline suited marines to minor tasks requiring the regularity that seamen lacked before continuous service. Hauling in the log, turning the sandglass and proclaiming the passage of time were responsibilities that lasted into the twentieth century. Marines became wardroom attendants (WRAs), keyboard sentries, lamp-trimmers, butchers and ships' postman. None of these jobs needed a trained marine, and ambitious officers regarded them with distaste. Marines continued to stand sentry until after the Second World War, senior officers issuing nervous reminders of the dangers of firing rifles in busy dockyards. Today the corporal of the gangway is commonly a naval rating, and may even be a woman.

3.2 Ashore

Royal Marines served ashore as well as at sea, creating different types of unit, with different records. The most common land-based formation was a temporary battalion created for some specific purpose, dissolved when no longer needed. Individual members of such units then rejoined their division, unlike early marines who were dismissed when their parent regiment was disbanded. The demands of total war in the twentieth century created larger RM formations, the RN and RM Divisions of the First and Second World Wars, and specialist heavy artillery units.

3.2.1 Battalions RM

Marines formed battalions to take part in military operations ashore that were beyond a ship's detachment. That might be because the projected operation was larger or more protracted than a ship's detachment could support, or because its naval component was slight. Marine battalions were obviously useful during combined operations, for example eighteenth-century landings on Belle Isle and Guadeloupe or the seizure of the Suez Canal in August 1882. Often they simply reinforced an over-stretched army, as they did at Bunker Hill in 1775. Less welcome was garrison duty in such far flung posts of empire as Wei-hai-wei on the Yellow Sea in the 1880s, where ponies shied at the mere sight of Europeans.

Marine battalions could be formed from fleet detachments under their own officers. The Mediterranean Fleet did this to support military operations in Egypt in 1800, and again in the Sudan in 1883. More commonly one or more divisions formed a battalion from officers and men at headquarters, like that at Belle Isle (1761), which traditionally won the laurel wreath that encircles the

Bad hair day at Yokohama: sergeants of the RM Battalion who served in Japan in the 1860s. The sentry on the left is wearing a white 'havelock' cap cover for protection against the sun.

Corps badge. Men of different divisions formed separate sub-units. RMA and RMLI constituted separate battalions in Egypt in 1882.

A battalion was commanded by a lieutenant colonel, sometimes a major. Eighteenth-century battalions had a nominal establishment of ten companies of 100 men each, but usually numbers were less. One embarked for Canada in 1759 had 24 officers, one surgeon, 21 sergeants, 16 drummers and 540 other ranks. The battalion embarked in HMS *Diadem* for operations off northern Spain in 1812 had 694 men in eight companies. First World War battalions numbered over a thousand at full strength, in four large companies lettered 'A' to 'D'. Second World War RM Battalion establishments fell to 690 other ranks, with four smaller rifle companies, a much larger headquarters and a new support company with 3in mortars, Bren carriers and assault pioneers.

Early marine regiments fought as battalions at Gibraltar (1704) and Cartagena (1741), but the great period for independent battalions was the nineteenth century. Marines were ideal for imperial emergencies, being able to move ten or a thousand miles at twelve hours' notice, and take care of themselves wherever they went. The table below lists nineteenth-century RM battalions and the campaigns or battles in which they engaged.

Area of Service	Date(s)	Conflict
Africa: Gold Coast	1873–4	Ashanti War
Africa: Zululand	1879	Zulu War
China: Canton	1838–42	1st China War (Opium War)
China: Canton	1856–58	2nd China War
China: Taku Forts	1858–60	3rd China War
China: Peking Legations	1900	Boxer Rebellion
Egypt: Alexandria	1800	French Revolutionary War
Egypt: Alexandria, Suez Canal	1882	Battle of Tel-el-Kebir
Japan: Simonoseki	1864	Anglo-French intervention
Japan: Yokohama	1870–75	Garrison
Mexico: Vera Cruz	1862	Diplomatic escort
North America: Washington, Great Lakes and New Orleans	1813–15	War of 1812
Portugal: Lisbon	1810–12	Peninsular War
Russia: Crimea	1854–5	Battles of Balaklava and Inkerman
Spain: Biscay coast	1812	Peninsular War
Spain: Biscay coast	1833–40	Carlist War: Battle of Hernani
Sudan: Suakin	1883–84	Battles of El Teb, Tamai, Tofrek
Syria: Beirut, Acre	1840	Intervention against Mehemet Ali

Numerous RM battalions were formed in the early twentieth century, now distinguished by numerals. Numbers were re-used, as units were dissolved and raised again. Today's RM Commandos are in effect permanently embodied battalions, removing the need for ad hoc RM battalions. The table below lists RM battalions formed between the world wars, showing where and when they served. The last column indicates the unit's function, its successor (e.g. '42 RM Cdo'), or controlling formation ('MNBDO I').

Designation	Date(s)	Area of Service	Notes
RM Field Force	1918–19	Murmansk, Archangel	Ski trained
RM Public Duties Bn	1935	London	Ceremonial
1st RM Bn	1940–3	Home, Dakar	42 RM Cdo
2nd RM Bn	1940–3	Home, Iceland, Dakar	43 RM Cdo
1st & 2nd RMLI Bns	1916–19	with RND	see 3.2.2
3rd RM Bn	1940–3	Home, Dakar	44 RM Cdo
3rd RMLI Bn	1916–21	Aegean, Bosphorus	
4th RM Bn	1918	Zeebrugge	
5th RM Bn	1918–19	Home	Mine clearing
	1940–3	Home, Dakar	45 RM Cdo
6th RM Bn	1919	Murmansk	Mutinied
7th RM Bn	1919	Schleswig	Plebiscite
	1941–4	Egypt, Sicily, Italy	48 RM Cdo
8th RM Bn	1920–2	Ireland	Coast guard
	1940–1	Home	41 RM Cdo
9th RM Bn	1918–21	Home	Coal strike
	1942–3	Home	46 RM Cdo
10th RM Bn	1921	Home	Coal strike
	1941–3	Home	47 RM Cdo
11th RM Bn	1921–3	Turkey	
	1940–4	Tobruk, India, Ceylon	MNBDO I
12th RM Bn	1927	Shanghai, Nanking	Legation defence
	1941–2	Home	MNBDO II

Designation	Date(s)	Area of Service	Notes
13th RM (Reserve) Bn	1920–1	Home	Coal strike
15th RM Machine Gun Bn	1940–3	Home	LCG crew
18th RM (Mobile) Bn	1940–4	Home	
19th RM Bn	1940–3	Scapa Flow	Coastal defence
20th–25th RM Bn	1940–4	Home	Training units
26th RM Bn	1944–6	Home	Bomb damage
27th, 28th, 30th RM Bns	1944–6	NW Europe	116 RM Brigade
29th Bn	1944–5	Home	see 3.3.4
31st–33rd RM Bns	1945	NW Europe	117 RM Brigade

The most famous of these was 4th RM Battalion, raised in February 1917 to attack the German U-boat base at Zeebrugge on the Belgian coast. Realistic training with ball ammunition, smoke floats, flares and bomb-throwing on Deal beach foreshadowed commando methods. Assault parties sailed in two Mersey ferries, *Iris* and *Daffodil*, and the old cruiser *Vindictive*, barricaded with splinter-proof mattresses, and armed with howitzers and mortars. They wore rubber-soled gym shoes, life belts and steel helmets, and carried Lewis guns, Mills bombs, flame-throwers and coshes.

The attack went in before dawn on St George's Day 1918, the men suffering heavy losses running alongside the Zeebrugge mole. Survivors scrambled ashore, climbing down the sea wall on hook ropes. Casualties clearing the mole were heavy, and the withdrawal signalled early. Total losses were 366 of 740 marines embarked. Survivors were despondent, but found themselves a star turn back at Dover. The raid failed to prevent U-boats using Zeebrugge, but boosted civilian morale after the German March offensive. George V recognized the battalion's collective bravery with two VCs, awarded by secret ballot to Captain Bamford RMLI and Sergeant Finch RMA.

RM battalions functioned like other infantry, producing military records, such as battalion order books, which record names of the sick or personnel movements. Quartermasters kept logbooks or returns dealing with supply matters. The National Archives holds some order books and other material for nineteenth-century RM battalions, as does the RM Museum, which also holds diaries and albums kept by members of many units listed above. As with naval actions, the general course of land campaigns is well documented. Field and Blumberg are a good starting point for RM battalions before 1919. Individual actions are less easy to establish, though the army was more liberal in naming marine officers than the navy. Official despatches appeared in the *Gazette*, the fuller originals being at the National Archives. Unit war diaries exist for both world wars at the National Archives, sometimes under Admiralty or War Office and DEFE call numbers.

Members of a battalion drawn from a fleet's detachments should appear in their ship's muster lists. The North Spain (1812) and Simonoseki (1864) battalions may appear in documents relating to HMS *Diadem* and *Conqueror*, the ships in which they were based. Once more, casualty lists are a useful if depressing source.

3.2.2 The Royal Naval Division

The RND is a forgotten epic of the First World War. The formation began as a half-baked improvisation, pursuing ill-defined objectives with derisory means. It became one of the British Army's most effective 'stormer' divisions.

The RND included both RN and RM personnel. Like other British infantry divisions of the period it had three brigades of four battalions, with supporting services. The marines' initial contribution was three RMLI battalions, one per division, and a fourth from the RMA, together constituting the Royal Marine Brigade. A Depot battalion soon replaced the RMA, the four RMLI battalions titled Chatham, Portsmouth, Plymouth and Deal. The Corps also provided engineering, transport and medical units (see section 1.5.1), and machine-gun and trench mortar companies.

The brigade landed briefly at Ostend in August 1914 to probe the open right flank of the German advance through Belgium, becoming the RND's Third Brigade on its return. The other two were formed from naval reservists left over after mobilizing the fleet. Known as Royal Naval Brigades these had nothing in common with the ad hoc naval brigades discussed in section 3.1.2. The RM Brigade returned to the continent in September, disembarking at Dunkirk on the 29th. Lacking transport, signals, entrenching tools or khaki uniforms it was apparently meant to distract the Germans. The only artillery was a few naval field guns manned by RMA gunners. On 3 October the marines went to reinforce Belgian forces at Antwerp, where the RN Brigades joined them. Unable to reply to merciless German shelling, Major General Archibald Paris RMA, General Officer Commanding (GOC), withdrew his division on the night of 8/9 October. Few marines were killed, but some 300 wandered into neutral Holland to be interned for the rest of the war.

The RND's next commitment was equally ill-conceived. Still half-equipped, the division was sent to Gallipoli in early 1915 to help knock Turkey out of the war. Strategic surprise was lost by ineffective naval bombardments, and the RND thrown in piecemeal to support landings at Cape Helles and Anzac Cove, named after the Australian and New Zealand Army Corps. Both sides' losses were shocking. A *Globe & Laurel* correspondent wrote that jumping into captured Turkish trenches was like jumping on a spring mattress, so thick were the bodies. Casualties and lack of artillery reduced the RND to a defensive role, its attenuated marine battalions amalgamated as 1st and 2nd RMLI Battalions (Chatham & Deal and Portsmouth & Plymouth respectively). Again the RND was evacuated under the noses of the enemy, re-embarking on 8/9 January 1916.

The division returned to France in May 1916, finally receiving its proper allocation of field artillery with 223 and 317 Brigades Royal Field Artillery (RFA). Re-christened 63rd (Royal Naval) Division, its infantry brigades were renumbered 188, 189 and 190. Since the Admiralty failed to provide replacements, naval personnel were concentrated in the first two, the RMLI in 188. The 190th Brigade consisted of army units: 7th Battalion, Royal Fusiliers; 4th Bedfords; 1st Honourable Artillery Company (HAC); and 10th Royal Dublin Fusiliers. Another army unit, The Artist's Rifles, joined in 1918.

The RND fought in four great battles on the Western Front in 1916 and 1917:

Battle	Offensive	Dates
Somme	Ancre: Beaumont Hamel	13–14 November 1916
Somme	Miraumont	17–18 February 1917
Arras	Arleux: Gavrelle Windmill	28–29 April 1917
Third Ypres	Second Passchendaele	26 October 1917

It took its objectives at Beaumont Hamel and Miraumont, contributing to the German withdrawal to the Hindenburg Line early in 1917. Distances advanced were small and casualties numerous, exceeding RM losses at Jutland everywhere except at Miraumont. 'Sepulchred Gavrelle' was the Corps' worst ever single day, two small battalions suffering at least 885 casualties. Between offensives trench warfare took its toll, wiring parties and trench raids adding to the daily wastage of sniping and shell fire. Battalions did not spend all their time in the line, however. A brigade might have two battalions in the forward trenches, another in support, and one in reserve. Spells in each might last a week or more, depending on circumstance. Periodically whole divisions left the line for rest and training.

The final year of the war was different. The German offensive of March 1918 drove the British Army back across the old Somme battlefields, until it rallied beyond the River Ancre. Heavy losses forced the RMLI battalions to amalgamate, 2nd Battalion, Royal Irish Regiment replacing 2nd RMLI. That summer the Allies began the Hundred Days of forgotten victories that forced Germany to sue for peace. Open warfare became the rule, progress measuring kilometres instead of yards. The RND began September by taking the Hindenburg Line, after a ten-mile night approach march, and ended by storming the Canal du Nord. The same night RM Divisional Engineers bridged the Canal de l'Escaut, ten kilometres further on. Returning from leave, Walter Popham found the advance 'so swift that we felt we would never catch up our units'. The RMLI fought to the last, taking more prisoners at Niergnies on 8–9 October than there were marines to guard them. The Armistice on 11 November found the battalion in Belgium, where it wintered, returning to England in May 1919.

Blumberg devotes four chapters to the RND and its supporting units (see section 1.5.1), listing gallantry awards and mentions in despatches, as well as divisional staffs. The Fleet Air Arm Museum is the place for RND personal records. War diaries at Kew include the RM Brigade and Chatham Battalion in WO95/4290 and 4291. Several RND veterans, though not marines, published accounts of their service, in particular Douglas Jerrold. Such is continued interest in the RND that it has its own periodical of that name. Anyone researching an ancestor in one of the RND's army battalions should consult military records or regimental histories.

3.2.3 Artillery brigades

The RMA's repository skills made it a valuable source of artillery reinforcements during the First World War, howitzer and anti-aircraft brigades in France, and smaller units worldwide. In the Second World War the Corps was committed elsewhere, its role as land gunners incidental.

a) Howitzer Brigade RMA

Reports of super heavy howitzers used by the Germans at Liège in August 1914 inspired the Admiralty to acquire a dozen 15in howitzers, firing a 1,400lb shell, to be operated by the RMA.

Each howitzer dismantled into six separate loads, and needed eleven trucks to move it. Individual gun crews numbered five officers and 83 other ranks each, plus naval surgeons and SBAs, about 1,000 men for the whole brigade. Many were civilians enlisted for their mechanical skills. Weapons deployed singly, being known as 'Grandmother'. They suffered various technical problems, the worst being their 11,000-yard range, which required them to be placed much nearer the front line than was desirable for such immobile weapons. One was abandoned during the German offensive of March 1918, and parts of another left behind. Very large shells proved ineffective against trenches, and their blast was too great near friendly infantry. Their main use was against targets behind enemy lines, such as artillery, observation posts or villages.

The 15in howitzer first saw action in France in March 1915, and took part in all the major offensives. One was shipped to Gallipoli, where there was no machinery to unload it. Blumberg gives a chronology, with extracts from detachment diaries. Total casualties were: 38 all ranks killed, 107 wounded, and 72 gassed, the brigade returning to Eastney for demobilization in June 1919. The National Archives holds some brigade diaries and the order book.

b) Anti-Aircraft Brigade RMA

This was formed at Eastney in November 1914 with cadres returned from Antwerp. Inspired by the armoured cars used there (see section 3.3.4) the brigade was armed with 2pdr pompom guns on armoured lorries.

The brigade had four batteries lettered 'A'–'D' with four equipments each. 'B' battery saw action first, in March 1915 near Dunkirk. Anti-aircraft gunnery was an undeveloped science, but the RMA were accustomed to moving targets, and made good shooting. Mobility was helpful as the short ranged 2pdr operated near the front line, attracting German counter-battery fire. Other batteries brought total establishment to 490, with a high proportion of NCOs, drivers and mechanics.

As the British share of the Western Front expanded, 'A', 'C' and 'D' batteries moved away from the coast, and were absorbed by the Royal Artillery. 'B' battery stayed near Nieupoort and Dunkirk, re-equipped with converted field guns and 3in high angle guns. Administered by the Admiralty, it worked with Allied troops along the coast, and enjoyed considerable independence. One section claimed ten kills, its CO's voice communication at the guns becoming the pride of the district. 'B' battery fired its last shots in October 1918, returning to Eastney the following January.

c) Miscellaneous artillery units (1914–18)

Small detachments of Royal Marines, never more than a few hundred strong, served as gunners in obscure corners of the First World War:

- Orkneys (September 1914–1919): defence of Grand Fleet's anchorage at Scapa Flow.
- Serbia (January–December 1915): defence of Belgrade.
- Egypt (October 1915–Autumn 1916): coastal defence of Alexandria.
- South Africa (October 1914–August 1915): occupation of German Southwest Africa (now Namibia).

- East Africa (January 1916–January 1918): occupation of German East Africa (now Tanzania).
- Nieupoort (February 1917–March 1919): Belgian coastal defence.

Most of these formations were armed with naval 4in and 12pdr guns moved by mules, oxen, lorries or African gun porters. The most significant was the RMA Heavy Siege Train in Belgium. The Royal Navy had installed heavy guns on the Belgian coast to counter German guns deployed there since 1914. The RMA took over in 1917, replacing naval personnel needed at sea. The May 1918 establishment included 427 NCOs and men RMA, manning three 12in guns, eight 9.2in, and six 7.5in on ship's mountings with concrete platforms. The gunners lived in bunkers underneath the sand dunes. Besides counter-battery fire, they supported the Zeebrugge raid (see section 3.2.1) and the final offensive of 1918, firing up to 33,000 yards. Low casualties were a tribute to the marines' skill in digging: 11 killed and 16 wounded. The unit returned to Eastney in March 1919.

d) RM Siege Regiment (August 1940–March 1945)
The RM Siege Regiment was formed after the fall of France in May 1940 to engage German targets in the Pas-de-Calais. The original battery was armed with two 14in naval guns emplaced on St Margaret's Bay golf course near Dover. The first gun was installed in the summer, the second in December. Meanwhile a second battery had been formed with three 13.5in guns on railway mountings. With a twenty-seven mile range these could trade shells with German heavy batteries across the Channel, although their primary target was the invasion. As invasion fears receded, numbers fell from 700 to 300, mostly HO recruits. They fired off all their ammunition supporting the Allied advance on Calais and Boulogne in September 1944. After that they retrained as infantry for 116 and 117 RM Brigades, or for 34 Amphibian Assault Regiment, bound for north-western Europe and the Far East respectively. Regimental headquarters disbanded in March 1945.

e) 5th RM Anti-Aircraft Brigade (March 1944–December 1945)
The MNBDO (see below) included many anti-aircraft units. Some escaped disbandment in February 1944 to become 5th RM Anti-Aircraft Brigade, with two heavy anti-aircraft regiments, one light regiment, a signals section and an operations room. In July and August the brigade deployed in south-east England, shooting down V1 flying bombs. They moved to Belgium in September, taking over air defence of the Scheldt estuary, including Antwerp, with numerous RA units under command. Communications were difficult, brigade signallers laying over 2,000 miles of telephone line between guns,

One of two 14in cross-Channel guns manned by the RM Siege Regiment in 1940, called 'Winnie' (after the Prime Minister) and 'Pooh'. This is 'Winnie'.

searchlights, smoke generators and ops rooms. The main threat was German secret weapons, the brigade logging 483 V1s and 313 V2s in the seven weeks to 12 December. The last air raid was on New Year's Day 1945, but V1 and V2 attacks continued until the brigade was relieved in March. It returned to the UK in May, disbanding in December 1945.

3.3 Combined operations

Marines have always taken part in combined operations, though they were not so named until the 1940s. Combined operations emerged from the Second World War, and the strategic need to re-enter German-occupied Europe without a friendly port. The original Royal Marine amphibious units, the MNBDO and RM Division, saw little action, but paved the way for more flexible units – commandos and landing craft flotillas.

3.3.1 MNBDO and RM Division

Mobile Naval Base Defence Organization or MNBDO dated from the 1920s when 'X' Organization experimented with landing craft and scaffolding piers on Eastney beach. In 1936, an 'MNBDO Nucleus' went to defend naval bases in Egypt and Palestine when Italy invaded Abyssinia (now Ethiopia).

MNBDO I was set up in 1939 to defend any ports the army might capture, but this never happened. Shipped to the Mediterranean in 1941, only 2,000 men out of 5,000 reached Crete before German airborne attacks began on 20 May. MNBDO anti-aircraft gunners fought until their guns were knocked out, before joining signallers and searchlight crews to fight as infantry. The Germans, however, had submachine guns, hand grenades and mortars, and were an uneven match for men armed only with rifles. Marines covered the retreat, and prevented a rush for the boats at Sphakia, but many were themselves left behind. MNBDO I then fortified islands in the Indian Ocean, or provided air defence for Egypt and Ceylon, until remustering as landing craft crew and infantry in 1944.

MNBDO II supported the Allied invasion of Sicily in 1943, providing signals, medical and security services, controlling malaria and unloading ships. 7th RM Battalion formed the basis for 31 Beach Brick, a beachhead infrastructure unit with engineer, signals, ordnance and medical units, plus an airfields group. Besides its logistic tasks, it fought as infantry on the Dittaino River, taking 150 prisoners. MNBDO II and 7th RM Battalion both returned home in 1944 for remustering.

The other amphibious striking force of the Second World War was meant to be the Royal Marine Division. It avoided being swallowed up by the army like the RND, but never saw action. Smaller ad hoc forces of Royal Marines occupied the Faroes in April 1940 (Sandall Force), and Iceland in May (Sturges Force). One of the few trained formations in the UK after Dunkirk the RM Division was committed to home defence, and then earmarked for secret operations, which never came off. An abortive attempt on the Vichy French enclave at Dakar in September 1940, with early-morning tea onboard passenger liners still on a peace footing, proved even more embarrassing. The ultimate disappointment was the invasion of Madagascar in May 1942, conducted with army units by General Robert Sturges RM, the RM Division's own GOC. The division disbanded a year later. The infantry mostly became commandos, the other units landing craft crews.

3.3.2 Royal Marine Commandos
Commandos were formed for short sharp raids, with an emphasis on light weapons and individual fighting skills. Their most significant combat role, however, has been as shock troops in battles of attrition. Royal Marines formed nine commandos during the Second World War:

Cdo	Formed	Theatres/Operations	Fate
40	1942	Dieppe, Sicily, Italy, Yugoslavia	Disbanded 1945
41	1942	Sicily, Italy, Normandy, Walcheren	Disbanded 1946
42	1943	Far East: Burma	Retained
43	1943	Italy: Comácchio, Yugoslavia	Disbanded 1945
44	1943	Far East: Burma	Renamed 40 Cdo 1947
45	1943	Normandy, Rhine/Weser crossings	Retained
46	1943	Normandy, Rhine/Weser crossings	Disbanded 1946
47	1943	Normandy, Walcheren; Holland	Disbanded 1946
48	1944	Normandy, Walcheren; Holland	Disbanded 1946

Most commando operations were amphibious, after a fashion. Most of 40 RM Commando never landed at Dieppe, the CO waving their assault craft away from an impossible beach, before being killed. Night assaults in Sicily by 40 and 41 were more successful, securing beachheads for standard infantry divisions. Four RM Commandos stormed ashore on D-Day, as part of the largest and most successful amphibious assault ever mounted. 46 RM Commando followed next day. Walcheren saw the first British use of armoured Landing Vehicles Tracked (LVTs) or 'Buffaloes', launched from landing craft to carry troops safely across fire-swept beaches. In Yugoslavia commandos operated with communist partisans, landing from motor launches and fishing boats behind German lines in the islands of modern

Royal Marine Commandos drive ashore from an LCT at Walcheren on 1 November 1944. Buffaloes lead the way, followed by smaller unarmoured Weasels.

Croatia. Lake Comácchio, 2 Commando Brigade's only operation as a formation, was described as, 'a nightmare mixture of Venice by Moonlight, and the end of the Henley Regatta transferred to a setting of mud, slime, and a few inches of stinking water'.

Once ashore, commandos fought as infantry. They became accustomed to close support from Canadian tanks in Normandy, and Indian armoured cavalry regiments in Burma, and more distant contributions from 25pdr field guns and supporting warships. At Lake Comácchio in April 1945 their difficulty was making use of all the supporting weaponry: field and medium artillery regiments, a radar unit, and an armoured menagerie of Buffaloes, Weasels, Kangaroos and DUKWs. Despite the Allies' material superiority, the battle came down to individual heroism. Corporal Tom Hunter, who charged three German machine guns firing a Bren gun from the hip, was killed drawing enemy fire away from his troop, to win the only Royal Marine VC of the Second World War.

Sometimes commandos were committed to protracted battles, hardly the role for which they were trained and equipped. 45 RM Commando was in Normandy for eighty-three days after D-Day. Autumn and winter 1944–45 found commandos miles inland patrolling the banks of Dutch and German rivers. Many ended the war on occupation duties, controlling displaced persons, arresting war criminals and chasing black marketeers.

All army and six Royal Marine Commandos were disbanded after the Second World War. Designations of the three surviving units changed from 'RM Cdo' to 'Cdo RM'. Their light infantry skills came into their own during the postwar retreat from empire. Marines became expert at hunting 'bandits' through Malaysian and other jungles, preparing meals without smoke, moving noiselessly, and going without cigarettes. 'X' Troop of 40 Cdo claimed the brigade's longest patrol in Malaya, twenty-two miles as the crow flies, but a three-week trip in the jungle. 45 Cdo RM ran a sideline in mountain warfare, chasing EOKA gunmen through the Troodos in Cyprus, and nationalist terrorists in Aden's Radfan. In Aden City every door and alley might represent danger or vital cover. Patrols inched along, two men at a time, learning skills soon needed closer to home in Northern Ireland.

Postwar operations depended almost exclusively on classic commando attributes of personal fitness, skill at arms and small unit tactics. Only at Suez in 1956 did the brigade conduct a set-piece landing, with LVTs careering down the streets of Port Said. So useful were commandos that two were reformed. 41 (Independent) Commando RM fought in Korea, as raiders and conventional infantry. Disbanded in 1952, 41 Commando RM reformed again in 1960, followed by 43 the following year. Both were disbanded again, in 1981 and 1968 respectively.

The individual and set piece strands of the commando inheritance came together during the Falklands War in 1982. Royal Marines formed the nucleus of the Crown's amphibious forces, providing landing craft crews and expertise, besides the core of an expeditionary force. Strategy took the place of LVTs, the expedition landing in San Carlos Water almost unopposed. Loss of a container ship loaded with helicopters put the emphasis back on individual fitness. Most of the infantry marched the 84 miles to Port Stanley, often carrying a total weight exceeding 120lbs. Closing in on the Argentinian defences, the British quickly established tactical superiority. Small patrol actions, often by night, prepared the way for close assaults with concentrated artillery and mortar barrages reminiscent of Second World War documentaries. One participant was reminded of *All Our Yesterdays*, 'hundreds of troops marching to the front, while artillery flashed on the horizon'.

Royal Marines continue to see action at both ends of the operational spectrum, sometimes as part of all arms task forces as in Iraq (2003), more often in lower intensity operations as in Kurdistan (1991), Sierra Leone (2000), Kosovo (2000), and Afghanistan (ongoing). A new organization known as Commando 21 incorporates new weapons such as .5in heavy machine guns, long-range sniper rifles, and 51mm mortars. Commandos now have two close combat and two standoff companies, instead of troops, besides command, logistic and base companies.

War diaries exist for Second World War Commandos under both ADM and DEFE call numbers. Record class ADM 202 covers Korea. Official records are not available for the Falklands or later. The *Globe & Laurel* contains extensive first-hand coverage of postwar operations, often illustrated with photographs. Few military organizations have been as heavily written up as the commandos, sometimes by authors who did not realize they were dealing with Royal Marines. The best starting points are Moulton and Thompson (see Further Reading). Ladd is thorough, but harder to read.

3.3.3 Landing craft

The British used landing craft in the 1750s. Flat-bottomed rowing boats propelled by sailors, they were no special concern of marines. The Corps became interested in landing craft in the 1920s: these were box-shaped craft with petrol engines, an armoured cab for the coxswain and a ramp at the bow. In 1938 the Inter-Services Training and Development Centre (ISTDC) moved into Fort Cumberland, with a Royal Marine adjutant. It developed many combined operations concepts, in particular the landing craft assault (LCA) intended to carry an infantry platoon, and the landing ship infantry (Large) or LSI(L) capable of launching many LCAs. Prototype LCAs were available three weeks before the Second World War began.

Fleet marines on exercise in 1957. Landing craft crews still wore blue berets, as here, with a red patch behind the globe and laurel badge. The marine on the left is wearing blue overalls.

The liberation of Europe required an armada of landing craft and men to operate them. The Royal Navy disliked running ships aground and was busy elsewhere. The RM Division and MNBDO were underused and ready for anything. When commandos absorbed the more military members of these formations, the majority remustered as crews for landing craft, organized in flotillas. Both ships and units were numbered. Ladd (pages 535–7) lists numbers identifying larger craft, and flotilla numbers for smaller ones.

Landing craft evolved for every amphibious need. Motor torpedo boats became landing craft infantry (small) or LCI(S), for high-speed raids. The need to land tanks and other vehicles inspired the landing craft tank (LCT). LCAs acquired a mortar and machine guns, becoming a landing craft support (medium) or LCS(M). After Dieppe, heavier craft were designed: landing craft support (large) or LCS(L) with anti-tank guns; landing craft gun (LCG) with either 25pdr guns or 4in gun turrets; LCT(R) with over 1,000 5in rockets. For anti-aircraft defence LCTs acquired 2pdr pom-poms and 20mm Oerlikons, becoming landing craft flak (LCF). Living conditions were poor, food tainted by the bilges, bulkheads dripping with condensation, men sleeping on tables, under tables and on the wash basins, seasick soldiers everywhere.

These craft and men made possible the landings in Sicily, at Salerno, Termoli and Anzio, and most notably in Normandy. D-Day flotillas represented the largest body of Royal Marines ever in action afloat, manning two-thirds of minor British landing craft. Landing craft covered the water in every direction, their diesel engines drowning out the bombardment. Flights of LCAs went flat out at nine knots through seas so high the coxswains had trouble finding the navigating leader's motor launch, squeezing between beach obstacles hung with land mines, to unload infantry onto the beach under a storm of mortar and machine-gun fire. Some were unlucky. One flight lost five LCAs out of seven in one trip.

LCFs stayed on after the initial assault, dissembled amongst other craft to ambush German bombers. After nightfall LCGs and LCFs formed the innocuous sounding but deadly 'Trout Line' to intercept human torpedoes and radio controlled motorboats, stuffed with high explosives, and heading for the invasion beaches. Several support craft were blown to bits before lookouts learned to lie on a mattress for a better angle of sight. The amphibious attack on Walcheren in the Scheldt estuary on 1 November 1944 saw the last of the LCGs and LCFs. With no room for manoeuvre, they tackled German batteries head on, pitting small calibre guns and lightly armoured vessels against some of the strongest defences in the world. After three and a half hours, only five of twenty-five support craft were still fit for action, but they had drawn the coastal batteries' fire, and the assault troops were ashore.

Royal Marines continue to man landing craft, on a much reduced scale. Purpose-built landing ships have replaced the LSI(L), which was usually a converted merchant vessel. Modern assault ships carry landing craft and helicopters and can 'flood down' to load tanks and heavy stores onto landing craft through doors at the stern. Known as Landing Platforms Dock (LPDs) these have been the basis of the Royal Marines' amphibious capability since the 1970s. HMS *Fearless* and *Intrepid* played a key role in the Falklands, justifying their replacement by a second generation named *Bulwark* and *Albion* after the commando carriers of the 1960s (see section 3.4).

Today, there are four Assault Squadrons RM, the organizational equivalent of a Second World War flotilla, assigned as follows:

	Attached to:
4 Asslt Sqn RM	HMS *Bulwark*
6 Asslt Sqn RM	HMS *Albion*
9 Asslt Sqn RM	HMS *Ocean*
539 Asslt Sqn RM	3 Commando Brigade RM

There is also a training unit, 1 Assault Group, based at Poole. The Corps currently operates three main types of landing craft:

- Landing craft utility (LCU) carrying a main battle tank, four vehicles or 120 infantry at twelve knots.
- Landing craft vehicle personnel (LCVP), carrying thirty-five troops or eight tons of stores or vehicles at twenty-five knots.
- Landing craft air cushion (LCAC) i.e. hovercraft, carrying sixty men.

The first two saw service in the Falklands, some LCUs carrying a Scorpion tank in pale imitation of an LCG. All three were used in Iraq.

3.3.4 Marines in tanks

Royal Marines have been associated with mechanized warfare since its beginnings. In September 1914 150 marines were assigned to 'Samson's Motor Bandits' to protect naval airfields near Dunkirk. They had a variety of vehicles, some armoured, mostly carrying machine guns. Commander Samson RN was in overall command, with Major Risk RMLI as his aptly named assistant. The motor bandits had several brushes with German cavalry, before convoying the RM Brigade to Antwerp in 'B' type buses (see section 3.2.2). Some cars saw action during the First Battle of Ypres, returning to England in November.

The Royal Marines' second venture into armoured warfare arose from preparations for D-Day. An Armoured Support Craft Group of five batteries were equipped with Centaur tanks to accompany the initial assault in LCTs, engaging German beach defences over open sights. The tank engines were removed, but later put back so the crews could drive ashore, and provide close support as the battle moved inland. Each battery had four troops of four Centaurs, with 95mm gun-howitzers and a Sherman tank for troop HQ, a total of 80 Centaurs and 20 Shermans. The group also included Royal Artillery and Royal Armoured Corps drivers and fitters, who were not marines. With a fully armoured turret the Centaur could be used further forward than the open-topped self-propelled guns of the day, though not for fighting other tanks. They can be recognized in photographs by their stubby guns and white numbers painted round the square turret to help direct their fire. RM crews wore blue berets with conspicuous Globe and Laurel badges. They withdrew on 24 June, the RA taking over the remaining tanks.

Survivors remustered as 29th RM Battalion, which in March 1945 became 34th RM Amphibian Support Regiment. This had two armoured batteries with standard LVTs, one rocket, and one flamethrower battery, mounted in adapted LVTs. Sent to South-East Asia the unit saw no action before the

Japanese surrendered. Subsequently they deployed to the Dutch East Indies (now Indonesia), returning home to be disbanded in 1946.

The Corps used their Second World War LVTs until they wore out. On switching to an Arctic role in the late 1960s, 3 Commando Brigade acquired Volvo BV202 tractors for use over snow. These have tracks like tanks, but are not armoured. Some saw active service in the Falklands. Since then commandos have used Warrior combat vehicles in Kosovo and the new Viking Armoured Vehicle in Afghanistan. Armoured Land Rovers mounting heavy machine guns have become standard, a more reliable incarnation of the motor bandits of 1914.

David Fletcher's *War Cars* discusses early armoured cars, while Blumberg describes their operations. The armoured support group is less well covered in secondary literature, but the National Archives has records of the amphibian support regiment's organization and training. The RM Museum has a photograph album of the regiment in India.

3.3.5 *Special forces*

The disciplined individualism of the Royal Marines makes them a natural recruiting ground for special forces units. About 40 per cent of British special forces today are Royal Marines.

Special Boat Section (SBS) descends from army commandos who used canoes for raids and intelligence gathering in occupied Europe. Their value as a source of beach survey data to an amphibious organization is obvious, and in 1945 they became part of the Royal Marines. SBS teams deployed to the South Atlantic during the Falklands War, and were the first formed troops into Kabul in 1991. The SBS is an extremely discreet organization. Family historians will do better looking for official records of any SBS ancestors before they transferred into the section.

Second World War special forces are also likely to disappoint the family historian, as they resembled suicide clubs, in particular the RM Boom Patrol Detachment (RMBPD), known as the Cockleshell Heroes. Small Operations Group (SOG) and RM Detachment 385 were based in the Far East, mounting raids behind Japanese lines. Viper Force ran armed motorboats on the Irrawaddy River during the British retreat through Burma in 1942. Only 48 of the original 102 MNBDO volunteers returned safely to India. 30th Assault Unit was a naval intelligence outfit who pushed ahead of the main battle to recover maps, codes and other material from recently vacated German headquarters. It included RN and RM personnel; among the former was Ian Fleming, James Bond's biographer.

3.4 Flying Marines

A family historian is more likely to find a marine ancestor guarding a Royal Naval Air Station than taking to the skies as aircrew. Nevertheless, Royal Marine fliers saw service in both world wars. Helicopters have become an essential form of transport between ship and shore, some flown by Royal Marines, others by Fleet Air Arm or RAF personnel.

The first four naval officers trained as pilots before the First World War included Lieutenant E L Gerrard RMLI who received his certificate on 2 May 1911, having previously qualified on airships. Army and navy had their own aviation wings then, the Royal Flying Corps (RFC) and Royal Naval Air Service (RNAS) respectively. Fifteen marine pilots and three observers flew with the latter. These small numbers fell after the RAF absorbed the RNAS in 1918. Establishment of an independent Fleet Air Arm in 1937, however, attracted more Royal Marines to the air service. Thirty-one RM pilots and two observers flew in action during the Second World War, and nine NCOs transferred to the Fleet Air Arm as rating pilots. Royal Marine dive-bomber pilots sank the German cruiser *Königsberg* on 10 April 1940, the first large warship destroyed by air attack in the Second World War.

The Royal Marines' most striking contribution to military aviation was 45 Commando's helicopter-borne assault on Port Said in 1956. Its success made helicopters an essential component of amphibious operations, landing troops, spotting for artillery, flying stores into forward areas, and removing casualties. Two aircraft carriers, HMS *Bulwark* and *Albion*, became commando ships, each carrying a complete commando with guns, vehicles, helicopters, and landing craft. Stood down after the withdrawal from east of Suez, commando ships have returned with the purpose-built *Ocean*, and the new *Albion* and *Bulwark*.

The Commando Brigade formed its own air squadron in 1968, with RM, RA and REME personnel. Flying Sioux, Gazelle and Scout helicopters they deployed to Norway, Belize and Kurdistan, and saw active service in Northern Ireland and the Falklands. In 1995 they became 847 Squadron based at Yeovilton, equipped with Lynx and Gazelles. The Commando Helicopter Force includes both RN and RM personnel, which have seen active service in Iraq and Afghanistan. Flying records of RM personnel should be sought at the Fleet Air Arm Museum ,Yeovilton.

3.5 Casualties

Wounds, sickness and death are inevitable accompaniments of war, their impact varying with the intensity of operations and the effectiveness of the medical help provided to those engaged.

3.5.1 Sick and hurt

Early marines were more likely to die of disease than enemy action. Battles were few and weapons inefficient. Campaigns lasted years, hygiene was rudimentary and medical knowledge limited. The Cartagena expedition in 1741 was destroyed by dysentery, malaria and yellow fever, not by Spanish bullets. Such diseases were not unknown nearer home. Sent to garrison Ostend, Bruges and Louvain against the French in 1678, the Admiral's Regiment suffered more from the ague than the enemy.

Marines were, 'a devilish expensive service' in the 1740s, with wastage rates far above line regiments. Admiral Anson complained his marines 'died like rotten sheep'. Unwashed and crowded together, ships' detachments rapidly fell victim to contagious diseases like 'the Itch' (scabies), or 'putrid fever' (typhus). John Howe was effectively treated for the former with 'hogg lard and brimstone' (sulphur in pig's fat), but the standard mercurial treatment for typhus was almost as dangerous as the disease. Captain Tooker Collins burnt clothing of men who died sailing to Canada in 1759, rather than auction it and spread the infection.

A contemporary summarized shipboard ailments as fever, flux, scurvy and 'an accidental evil, the Small Pox'. He knew scurvy came from eating salt provisions, but blamed the West Indian climate for the first two, in line with current epidemiological theory. Despite improvements in naval medicine, a marine battalion of 1814 buried its surgeon and sixty more on the short passage from Chesapeake Bay to Cumberland Island, Georgia. Only at the end of the nineteenth century did naval hygiene manuals recognize the mosquito's role in malarial fevers and of human waste in diseases such as dysentery. Perhaps because wastage was so high, *Admiralty Instructions* devote numerous paragraphs to the administrative care of sick and hurt marines, ensuring their kit and weapons accompanied them to hospital, and making arrangements for their subsequent return to headquarters. If the treatment of sick marines remained problematical, at least they need not get lost.

One reason the First World War appears so terrible is that for the first time battle casualties outnumbered deaths from disease. Fighting was more intense, with fewer intervals between engagements, and weapon technology was more deadly. Total numbers of Royal Marines killed or wounded in action between 1914 to 1919 were 6,371 and 6,498 respectively, against 1,057 who died of disease. Comparable figures at Gibraltar in December 1704 were 87 dead, 189 wounded and 333 sick, although some of these would have recovered. About 10 per cent of Royal Marines wounded during the First World War subsequently died, a better survival rate than after Bunker Hill, when Lieutenant David Collins commented 'they die so fast of their wounds that nobody as yet has got a true state of our loss'. Modern medicine keeps marines fit, until they become battle casualties, and then gives them a better chance of recovery. In the Falklands not a single friendly casualty died after reaching the Medical Squadron at Ajax Bay.

Sea battles under sail were not risk free, and marines were particularly exposed on the upper decks. At the First Battle of the Capes in 1781 John Howe 'was Stationed on the forecastle with twelve Privates 2 Corporal 1 Serjent and one Lieutenant of marines . . . they were all killed and wounded except myself and too Privats and the Lieut' (*sic*). Royal Marines made up 15 per cent of British numbers at Trafalgar, but suffered 36 per cent of the killed and wounded. Lewis Rotely was the only one of *Victory*'s marine officers to escape Trafalgar uninjured.

Early medical care was not always ineffective. John Curtis, of Holt's Regiment, was shot through the head at Gibraltar, with 'several pieces of his Scull taken out', and lost his left arm at Alicante in 1706, but he survived to petition for relief six years later. Twenty-six marines died of wounds after Trafalgar, against 271 wounded, a similar proportion to the First World War. Psychological casualties seem to have received little help, however. The senior major to survive Bunker Hill died 'not of any wound but of an absolute Penury and narrowness of Soul, which brought on a Flux'. Hannah Snell, the female marine, died in Bedlam.

From the 1690s, sick and hurt marines were treated by naval surgeons and sick berth attendants in naval hospitals. While serving ashore as part of the army they would be cared for by RAMC personnel. The first RAMC other rank to win the VC was Lance Corporal Henry Harden, killed as a troop medical orderly with 45 Commando in 1945. Divisional headquarters also had their infirmaries. The Woolwich Infirmary Establishment is at Kew under ADM 104/3. Naval hospital musters for 1740 to 1869 are held under ADM 102. Marines wounded in twentieth-century conflicts may appear in war diaries for army hospitals and regimental aid posts, WO 95 and WO 169 for the First and Second World Wars respectively. Records of evacuation to hospital ships in both wars are in WO 222. The National Archives also holds admission and discharge registers for 2nd General Hospital for Royal Marines 1918 (MH 106/986–997). Medical history sheets for First World War marines are at the Fleet Air Arm Museum, and are open to next of kin. Otherwise, only a small percentage of medical records has survived. The run down in service hospitals has resulted in wounded marines being treated in National Health hospitals, with dubious consequences both for them and future family historians.

3.5.2 *Prisoners of war*

The fate of prisoners of war, abbreviated 'POW' or 'pw', depends on their captors. European standing armies of the eighteenth century rarely killed prisoners once their surrender had been accepted. Their maintenance, however, remained their own responsibility or that of their government. Queen Anne's reign saw complex arrangements for exchanging marines captured in Spain and elsewhere, or passing them money. Even in revolutionary situations, as in the American War of Independence, prisoners were looked after or exchanged. Receipts were given for any imbalance in numbers, to be adjusted subsequently.

Standards declined in the Napoleonic Wars. Captain Richard Swale noted the poor condition of some captured marines returned in 1801, 'several of them bad of their wounds, many others had died in the French Hospital, they were almost naked, and several had not been shaved (or I suppose washed) from the time they were made prisoners'. Marines captured at Buenos Aires in 1807, were marched deep into Argentina, and despaired of ever seeing home. They were physically free, however, unlike French prisoners in British hulks. Guarding these was one of the contemporary marine's most disagreeable duties, many returning to headquarters with shattered health.

Royal Marines captured in both world wars were ostensibly protected under the Geneva Convention. In Germany they faced slow starvation, fed a daily basin of hot water with two or three runner beans floating on top, with perhaps a potato for their midday meal. Hitler's Commando Order of October 1942 specified death for captured commandos. Among those subsequently murdered were four of the RMBPD. One in five marines captured by the Japanese never returned. A list of Royal Marines held in German prisoner of war camps 1939–45 is at ADM 201/111.

3.6 Termination of service

This section logically follows the above discussion of the risks incurred by Royal Marines, and concludes Chapter 2's analysis of their administration. Marines left the service in several ways. The significance accorded these was not necessarily the same as it would be today. Desertion tempted the most reliable marine, as the only way out of service at a time of his choosing. A pension was not always the likely end of a sea soldier's career.

3.6.1 Length of service
Early marines did not sign on for a fixed period. Other ranks enlisted for 'life', modified to two twelve-year terms in 1847, the second later reduced to nine. Total service might still exceed twenty-one years, as years before a man's 18th birthday did not count, and men overseas might serve longer. Shorter terms also occurred, as with twentieth-century national servicemen. Today the Corps provides flexible career structures (FCS), from six months upwards.

Until 1757 marine officers might sell their commissions when they liked. After the abolition of purchase, they grew old in the service, with effects discussed in section 2.3.2. Major J Uniacke, who died of sunstroke in China in 1842, was first commissioned in 1804, thirty-eight years earlier. Other ranks rarely served so long. Few eighteenth-century marines lasted more than twelve years, before falling victim to infirmity or death. Enhanced longevity in the nineteenth century allowed increasing numbers to complete their twenty-one years. As the upper age limit for enlistment was 26, few Victorian marines would have served beyond their 50th birthday, however. Meanwhile the government began forcing officers to retire at an age dependent upon rank, 42 for a captain in 1878 or 65 for a general. Today's FCS allows service up to age 55.

3.6.2 Discharge by purchase

The only legal exit for other ranks before 1847 was discharge by purchase. Payments varied with the cost of providing two replacements, which went up in wartime. Ten guineas in 1772 became forty in the 1790s. Nevertheless, fifty-nine men bought themselves out of Portsmouth Division during the first five months of 1800. Later regulations set a tariff based on service and Good Conduct Badges. In 1884 a man with no GCBs and less than seven years might pay £30, reducing to £4 after sixteen years, and nothing after seventeen. In 1945 rates were £48 in the first four years falling to £24 after six. Recruits of less than three months paid just £20. Given inflation, therefore, the cost had fallen considerably.

Discharge by purchase was not automatic, and permission might be refused. A thirty-day cooling off period applied in cases of free discharge, during which any pension implications would be explained. Nevertheless, men left in the most arbitrary manner. In 1868 a Sergeant Taylor bought himself out two years short of pension, to avoid going to Malta. On the other hand, John Hopkinson took a cruise in the hungry 1840s, and bought his discharge on his return, thinking he could find a better market for his labour. The words 'SOLD OUT' on description books and service papers show a man purchased his discharge. The National Archives hold a few books listing discharges by purchase, kept by the Marine Pay Office, while individual cases may appear in divisional letter books.

3.6.3 Death in service

Eighteenth-century officers' widows received pensions, £16 for an ensign's relict in 1746, up to £50 for a colonel's. Other ranks' dependants were thrown into despair, made worse by official communications that named officer casualties, but not other ranks. All they could hope for was any money left from the traditional auction 'at the mast' of a dead man's effects, after paying his debts to the Crown. Pensions for other ranks' dependants date from 1883, starting at 5*s* a week, and rising to 9*s* for a colour sergeant, plus 1*s* 6*d* to 2*s* per dependant child. A widow's pension was suspended on remarriage (excluding the children). A widow on parish relief received nothing. Widows might also receive a gratuity equal to their husband's full pay for a year.

Death generates paperwork. When a marine died at sea, the captain sent a certificate to headquarters, where divisional records such as description books were annotated 'DD' for discharged dead. Official records include:

- Registers of deaths in ships since 1893 (ADM 104/109–21). The last seventy-five years are closed, but indexes are available.
- Registers of killed and wounded 1854–1929 (ADM 104/144–9), indexed from 1915 (ADM 104/140–3).
- The war grave roll (ADM 242/7–10) lists First World War deaths alphabetically, as do Navy Lists for early months of that conflict.

An Edwardian postcard preserves the pomp of a military funeral. A marine ancestor is more likely to feature at such events in a supporting role than as the central attraction.

- Registers of reports of deaths of naval ratings 1939–45 (ADM 104/127–39) includes Royal Marines killed in the Second World War.

The Royal Marines Museum and National Archives hold copies of Captain Good's registers of Royal Marines' war deaths for both world wars. Obituaries for officers may be found in the *Globe & Laurel*, newspapers, or mid-nineteenth-century obituary books at the National Archives (ADM 1/51–2 and 6/448). Brief notices may appear in the *Gentleman's Magazine, Annual Register*, or *Army and Navy Gazette*.

Records of pensions awarded officers' widows and children are held under ADM and PMG call numbers, from 1712 and 1837 respectively; those of other ranks' dependants from 1870. Children may appear in Registers of Powers of Attorney (1800–99). Marines' wills and letters of administration (1740–64) are collected in ADM 96/254. Other ranks' wills deposited at the RN Pay Office are in ADM 48, indexed at ADM 142.

3.6.4 Invaliding out

Wounded officers were entitled to assistance, depending on their injuries, the circumstances and how much influence they could mobilize. Captain William Pridham merely suffered 'a contraction of the muscles of the right leg caused by a check of perspiration', but was retired on full pay in 1815. More severe injuries might not result in leaving the service. Captain John Mason of Will's Regiment was still at sea, despite losing an arm at Gibraltar, when he petitioned for a post as lieutenant governor of Carlisle Castle in 1711.

Marines 'worn out' after their twenty-one years could apply to the Royal Hospital at Greenwich like disabled seamen, but demand for places outstripped supply. In the late 1790s, Portsmouth Division discharged at least fifteen marines a month as unfit, compared with a few thousand places at the hospital. Following the Napoleonic Wars, other ranks were told 'on no consideration to trouble the Lords of the Admiralty respecting pensions unless absolutely worn out in the service, so as to be rendered incapable of labour'. Chatham Chest was another overstretched source of help. John Curtis of Holt's Regiment had received £7 after his many wounds, but in 1711 the Chest had been 'stopt three years next Christmas', the officers not paying their contribution. Injured marines might also appear in Poor Law records. Thomas Hoole, of Shovell's 2nd Marine Regiment, was reduced by injuries to teaching 'petty scholars' at Upper Rawcliffe in Lancashire. The guardians gave him and his family thirteen pence a week, 'for they think it no sin to slyte a poor man'.

The Victorians put matters on a sounder footing, with a tariff of pensions for severe wounds or hurts. Daily rates for a private in 1862 ranged from 8*d* or 1s for a man still able to work to 2s for loss of two limbs or both eyes. Loss of a left eye did not render him unfit for service, but loss of a right eye did, reflecting the importance of marksmanship. Specific provision for cases of rupture recall the continued importance of hard physical work in the Victorian navy. Men injured on service were sent home with a statement of their case for consideration by a board of senior medical officers. Surveys for invaliding were usually held at naval hospitals at Chatham, Haslar in Gosport, Portland, Plymouth and South Queensferry near Rosyth, as best suited the applicant. Medical reports were confidential, and eventually passed to the Admiralty. Following the First World War an Order in Council of 8 May 1919 granted disabled sailors and marines permanent pensions on the same basis as soldiers, paid by the Ministry of Pensions.

3.6.5 Desertion

Desertion was commonplace among early marines, running away from an unkind employer being just part of Stuart and Georgian civil life. Some deserted to earn further bounties by re-enlisting. A soldier shot in Hyde Park in 1744 had made over £100. Others simply sought fresh employment. A deserter entering the *Kinsale* as a seaman in 1705 asked the captain to intercede for him, 'he having resolved never to live in the marines any longer'. Reliable men might succumb to a sudden chance of freedom. Captain Wybourn lost four of his best men in 1813, who had themselves been sent to bring in some stragglers. Desertion was not restricted to the lower orders. Second Lieutenant George Nairn of the 25th Company was 'Dismissed the service for Desertion from the "Augusta" 1 November 1765'.

Official responses to desertion were ambiguous. Amnesties offered pardons for those who returned. Advertisements offering rewards for apprehending those who did not provide rare descriptions of working-class men, like this from the *London Gazette* in 1709:

> John Grindle, a lusty black man, having a bushy Head of Hair, very much pitted with the small pox, somewhat round shouldered, Richard Hill a lusty man of a fair complexion, having lank hair, he goes creeping with his Feet.

Wages were withheld, or paid in arrears to deter desertion, to little effect. When John Brooks ran from Chatham in May 1806, he abandoned all the pay he had accrued since *Victory* paid off in January.

A deserter's entry in the muster roll of his ship was marked 'R' or 'Run', although in an age of poor communications many cases seem to have been technical. At Portsmouth a man found north of Kingston was considered a deserter, without his ever leaving Portsea Island. In cases of overrun leave or poor time-keeping, the man's record was corrected on his return to duty. Otherwise a deserter faced court martial, with potentially fatal consequences (see section 2.3.3). Divisional order books often name deserters when detailing an escort to bring them back. John McCarthy of Portsmouth Division appears twice: first on 8 September 1799 being retrieved from the Savoy prison in London, then on 7 October, 'to Receive the remainder of his Punishment'. But the details of such cases must be sought in the court martial records.

3.6.6 Dismissal

John Coale was freely discharged from the Duke's Regiment in 1676 having had 'the good luck to have an estate fallen on him lately'. Less fairytale endings to their careers befell John Wilkinson, 'a brisk young man', discharged in 1705 for 'a defect in one eye', and Peter McClachlen, dismissed in 1790 for lacking 'capacity to learn any part of his Duty'.

More commonly dismissal followed some clash with authority. Lieutenant George Brunette was struck off in 1800 'for Neglect of Duty, in absenting himself from Head Quarters without leave'. Other officers of the period were dismissed for consorting with a 'Lady of the Town', or drinking with common soldiers, 'most ungentlemanlike'. Dismissal often followed physical punishment. Isaiah Bayes, a Portsmouth recruit, demanded a general court martial for desertion in 1766, saying he would 'suffer death rather than be Floggd'. Sentenced to 1,000 lashes, he received 600 before being drummed out of the service. Queen Victoria's hard bargains faced gaol instead of flogging, their kit sold off on the public account. A marine discharged with ignominy when overseas might await the first government ship home, or be landed in a colony, which might give the Antipodean researcher an unpleasant surprise. A mutilated service record with the top corner cut off suggests an enforced departure from the Corps.

The most common form of dismissal accompanied the reductions following every major war. Divisions paraded for inspection by the commandant and surgeon, men over 40 or unfit being first for discharge. Those with most sea time or most debts were given priority for retention. The rest settled their accounts with the quartermaster and drew twenty-one days' pay for the journey home, keeping their clothes and knapsacks, but not side-arms. Early disbandments were less orderly. In 1699 marines refused to be disarmed until paid. Will's Regiment mutinied on Christmas Eve 1713, marching on London with colours flying and drums beating to protest against the depredations of the regimental agent. More restrained protests followed the abolition of Woolwich Division, redundant marines parading Whitehall with sandwich boards.

3.6.7 Pension

Pensions for long service were not generally available until the mid-nine-teenth century. The first marines to receive pensions on the basis of age, rather than wounds or gallantry, were twenty-four officers retired on full pay in 1792, to make way for younger men. Such retirements remained discretionary, until chronic congestion in senior and middle ranks compelled the Admiralty to retire older officers from the 1850s onwards. Annual pensions varied from £225 for a captain to £600 for a full colonel.

Other ranks first received retirement pensions after the 1847 Marine Act set a definite term to their engagement. Amounts were small, but more than most civilians received before Lloyd George's Old Age Pension of 1908. A private's basic rate in 1913 was 8*d* a day, plus a penny per Good Conduct Badge, another for the Long Service Medal, and another for being consistently awarded a 'very good' character. Senior NCOs received up to 3*s* a day, or more for those recommended for distinguished conduct or lengthened sea service. The new pensions did not apply to those who returned to civilian life before 1847. David Newton, a veteran of Trafalgar, was the object of public charity in 1873, when an old marine general assisted the village rector to get him a Greenwich out-pension of 1*s* 6*d* a day. HO marines of neither world wars were eligible for pension unless they subsequently transferred to continuous service.

Records of marine pensioners at Greenwich are with those of naval personnel in ADM 165–6. Officers receiving Greenwich Hospital pensions between 1862 and 1908 are listed in ADM 201/22 and 23, while retired pay records from 1871 to 1923 are in ADM 22/475–487. More recent records are held by the Director of Naval Personnel (see Chapter 4). Among the documents handed to a pensioner by his CO were a statement of service, discharge certificate, WRA's history sheet and National Insurance cards. Where they have survived these provide a wealth of detail about a man's service life.

Chapter 4

SOURCES – WHERE AND HOW TO FIND OUT ABOUT MARINES

4.1 How to trace your RM ancestor

In common with the humble foot soldier's barrack room humour, in research terms a dead bemedalled officer is a good thing! His promotions are recorded, his medals gazetted and his demise lamented with a plausible obituary. In short, he has more written about him. Unfortunately, the lowly marine, who signs on in times of comparative peace or survives shot and shell without a scratch, itch or lash can leave us with little: an attestation, service record and discharge certificate if we are lucky. That could, and sometimes is, the end of the matter, if it were not for the family – before, the Corps, and the descendants.

When discovering that an ancestor has served as a marine, the start point for research will vary from family to family, as will the generation of the ancestor in question. For many delving into their family history the character will often be within living memory, such as a grandfather; to others he may be generations back in a branch of a family tree already researched in name but not detail. Often the start point is a uniformed photograph in a family album, a group of medals framed over granddad's mantelpiece, or a tin in the attic containing buttons and a blue or manila OHMS envelope with folded service and discharge certificates. Armed with this type of source, the novice researcher will soon be able to add, if not understand, further information which will encourage the idle hobby into an obsession. Others will not have such an easy start, such as those furnished with few tangible facts other than a Christmas card sent from Stonehouse Barracks, and 'John Smith RM' engraved on a cigarette case. But a start can be made from even this meagre evidence.

Apart from the periods of conscription starting in 1916, 1939 and national service in 1947, most Royal Marines had chosen to be Royal Marines and thereby entered into a Corps that generated a strong family tradition and a 'once a marine, always a marine' ethos. Even those who enlisted as 'Hostilities Only' in the two world wars, or volunteered to do their national service in the Royal Marines, could not remain unaffected by the identity it afforded them – and this, for the family historian or genealogist, increases the likelihood of a legacy of material, memoir and souvenir being hoarded.

On the other hand the culture of official record collection in the last two centuries and the establishments that now administer access to them have changed dramatically, especially since the latter 1990s. Prior to that decade it could be said that the nature of the demand for public documents suited the retrieval point being by 'event'. Since that date the emphasis has shifted to the point being 'people', and family history centres came to reflect the increasing demand from people interested in genealogy. Record offices and archives are now far more open to the novice or enthusiast undertaking their own research, either in person or online.

An alternative to the naval and military route into the discovery of a Royal Marine ancestor is the unexpected appearance of 'RM' after a name on a civil document such as a birth, death or marriage certificate, or in a census record. With many census returns now online, many people are initiating their interest via this medium. However, there are pitfalls to be aware of. Whilst the typical census return offers a snapshot of address, location, name, family and profession of the recorded head of family, care is required with the latter

Royal Marines were family men: Sergeant S J Skinner with his wife and daughters in the 1920s. Besides three First World War medals, he wears a Naval General Service Medal (left) and Long Service Good Conduct Medal (right).

column to prevent a wasted avenue of research being entered into. For example, 'marine' can be mercantile marine, or a form of 'mariner' which in turn has, in some cases, been a wrongly entered 'marine'. A census entry alone will not necessarily provide a wealth of leads into naval and military records; the same being true of just a name and a date of birth.

4.2 The Internet

The global growth of the Internet has encouraged many people into tracing their family history, as it is a subject that lends itself to the medium. Record offices, archives, libraries and museums produce catalogues of their holdings as a matter of course, and were perhaps one of the first cultural sectors to embrace computer technology in its early days as a tool for assisting in this task. However, it should be remembered that these early systems were generally for the internal use of the individual establishment; the concept of linking collections, sharing data and public access to catalogues and databases was a long way off. It must be considered that not every institution the researcher may fall upon for records will have anything like their total holdings, or even their catalogues, available electronically. The migration of information held, for example, on a card index, into a searchable online database, can be a herculean task for a small and lightly staffed museum, for instance, and whilst financial assistance from governing bodies, grants, and Heritage Lottery Fund bids are helping in this area, be prepared to expect to visit and undertake your own research in the old-fashioned way.

Another point to consider is the quality of the information that can be found on the web. Entering 'Royal Marines' into an Internet search engine such as Google or Yahoo will produce in excess of 1,580,000 entries, some of which will be major sites, others merely the words themselves. Anyone with basic computer skills can produce a webpage, and such pages can be hosted for very little, or sometimes no cost. The 'surfing' Royal Marines researcher will come across many pages that pertain to one enthusiast's opinion or an ex-marine's memoir, but the mere use of the Globe and Laurel badge (often used illegally) can sometimes hint at official approval or accuracy of content.

With a little experience these types of sites will become apparent and the researcher will be faced with either searching an online catalogue, or viewing online documents. The latter activity may involve pay-to-view or download material, for which purchase by online credit or debit card is a usual method. Some sites will offer a system called Pay-Pal or World-Pay. All the payments are made to these systems themselves, who then pay the download site on your behalf. This can offer better security since the customer gives their details to only one site. It also enables safe purchases from smaller traders who may not have card facilities.

For further detail on the use of the Internet for family history in general see Peter Christian's *The Genealogist's Internet* (The National Archives: 2005) and also Simon Fowler's *A Guide to Military History on the Internet* (Pen & Sword: 2007).

4.2.1 A selection of some useful websites and e-mail addresses

- General current Royal Marines information, www.royal-marines.mod.uk
- Official Royal Marines regimental site, www.royalmarinesregimental.co.uk
- The *Globe & Laurel* (Corps magazine) royalsmag@btconnect.com
- MOD Information & Library, e-mail Info-LibsvcsGroupMailbox@defence. mod.uk
- Medal citations *London Gazette*, www.gazettes-online.co.uk
- The National Archives, www.nationalarchives.gov.uk & enquiry@nationalarchives.gov.uk
- National Maritime Museum, www.nmm.ac.uk
- The *Blue Band* (RM Band magazine), www.royalmarinesbands.co.uk
- The British Library Newspaper Library, newspaper@bl.uk
- Military Minded (personnel website), info@milmind.com
- Society of Genealogists guide to researchers, www.sog.org.uk
- Association of Genealogists in Archives, www.aga.org.uk
- Commonwealth War Graves Commission, www.cwgc.org
- 20th Century 'Scots at War', www.scotsatwar.org.uk
- Medal Identification, www.medals.net
- Imperial War Museum, www.iwm.org.uk
- Trenches on the web site, www.worldwar1.com
- Men who served at Trafalgar, www.genuki.org.uk/big/eng/Trafalgar
- Births Deaths & Marriages England & Wales since 1837, www.1837online.com
- Public Record Office of Northern Ireland, www.proni.gov.uk
- National Archive of Scotland, www.nas.gov.uk
- Veterans Agency MOD, www.veteransagency.mod.uk
- The National Army Museum, www.national-army-museum.ac.uk
- National Register of Archives, www.nra.nationalarchives.gov.uk/nra/
- Unit Histories is an ongoing ambitious site that attempts to provide unit histories of the Second World War, with biographies of the commander, www.unithistories.com

Please note: while the authors offer notification of the websites contained in the above list, they cannot be held responsible for accuracy of the information or quality of any services offered.

4.2.2 *Archive catalogues*

It is useful at this point to consider what type of information may exist and where it may reside when tracing records of a Royal Marine ancestor. There is a difference in the type of material that a record office will hold, and that which a museum will collect, for example. Official organizational, institutional and statistical records are more likely to be found in a national archive or county record office, while a personal diary, private papers or service ephemera would be an acceptable donation to an appropriate museum.

Not all museums have an archive as such, and the collection of any documents can be by sample and specimen for potential display purposes, rather than a continuity of records for study. While libraries, information centres and websites will usually consist of secondary sources, their retrieval aids, indexes and searchable databases can provide a rapid access to material. The catalogues of primary sources at record offices, archives and museums, either manual or electronic, can detail a resource, but may also interpret to a lesser degree.

With regard to the official records of the Royal Marines, selected records up to the period when the Royal Marines ceased to have their own discrete headquarters in 2002 (HQRM Portsmouth) are archived, and at the thirty-year point they are reviewed and go to either the National Archives or the Royal Marines Museum. At the time of writing (January 2008) the thirty-year period is under review for all MOD records. The archiving of current Royal Marine unit records continues, with release at the thirty-year point, dependent on security considerations. Records pertaining to Northern Ireland are not released for seventy-five years, along with personnel and courts martial records.

4.3 Key repositories and how to access them

The following is a list of repositories that contain material that would generally assist researchers of Royal Marines genealogy; it is not exhaustive, and institutions such as the National Army Museum, for example, will have sources relating to Royal Marines, as will probably every county record office in the country. To gain details of all record offices the researcher should check the ARCHON directory and the National Register of Archives; both can be accessed from www.nra.nationalarchives.gov.uk/nra/.

It should be noted that some of the offices described can only be accessed by next of kin, given the nature of the personnel detail they hold. Likewise other institutions have to operate an appointment system, so please check before writing a lengthy request or visiting unannounced.

The National Archives
The National Archives is the principal repository of official records of the Royal Marines reviewed under the Public Records Acts for retention. Amongst the classes of records are personal service records and official unit diaries made available to the public once the various time restrictions for certain records have lapsed.

The National Archives
Ruskin Avenue
Kew
Richmond
Surrey
TW9 4DU
0208 8876 3444
www.nationalarchives.gov.uk

The Royal Marines Museum Archive & Library
Access to the archive and library is by prior appointment only. E-mail enquiries will receive an automatic acknowledgement that will also give guidance information and a list of downloadable guides on frequently requested subjects. These guides are reviewed and added to, so it is worth checking the museum website for any updates. The library consists of 17,000 volumes and journals, dating from 1643 to the present day. The collection includes Navy Lists from 1783 to date, Marine Officers' Lists 1755 to 1886 and Army Lists dating from 1739. The books cover campaigns, military and naval social history, amphibious warfare, acts, orders and regulations, Marine Corps of other nations, ships and landing craft, music, biographies, medicine, law, casualty lists, weapons, vehicles, medals, uniform, barracks and locations. The journals consist of historical publications such as the *United Services Journal* from 1829 to 1870, *Naval Chronicle* 1799 to 1818 and a run of the *Annual Register* from 1758 to 1843. The library also holds the standard Royal Marines' histories and copies of the works listed in Further Reading.

The archive holds biographical records of certain non-commissioned ranks of the Royal Marines. These are confined to names that have been cross-referenced for reasons such as awards for gallantry, obituaries, correspondence or presentation of items to the museum. In addition, a *Register of the Regimental Sergeants Major, RM* has been compiled by former WO1 J A Forster RM (Corps RSM), which contains details of all known men of this rank, with the exception of those in the SBS.

The museum archive also contains a ships' detachment section of its catalogue (Arch 2/19 to 2/24) in which ship files, under name, contain material relating to the marines onboard. In the case of vessels sunk or damaged by enemy action, casualty and survivors lists are often included, originating from the divisional headquarters. Other lists of casualties and prisoners of war are to be found in the Arch 16/1/4 and Arch 15/15/1–8 series. There is a copy of the original casualty ledger for 1939–1945 (Arch 16/1/4). This records similar details to ADM 242 (see 4.5.2) with the addition of land unit or shore base location, and also deaths by accident and 'natural causes'.

Any research that has been undertaken by the museum in answering enquiries is also filed and indexed and can be retrieved usually by name, but in some cases by ship, unit or operation. This correspondence dates back to around 1965. Since the museum was founded in 1958, service records, and also officers' commissioning certificates, have been regularly donated to the museum archive. These are indexed and filed alphabetically by name; Arch 9/2/A-Z for officers and Arch 10/2/A-Z for ranks.

Royal Marines Museum
Southsea
Hampshire
PO4 9PX
02392 819385 selecting 6
E-mail: archive@royalmarinesmuseum.co.uk
Website: www.royalmarinesmuseum.co.uk

Personnel records for former Royal Marines
The service records of former Royal Marines before the progressing release date of 1928 are at TNA, Kew, and are open to the public. Those records awaiting review and transfer to Kew (currently 1928–38) are archived at the following address and can only be accessed by the subject or the next of kin, if dead.

Directorate of Personnel Support (Navy)
Navy Search
TNT Archive Services
Tetron Point
William Nadin Way
Swadlincote
Derbyshire
DE11 0BB
Tel: 01283 227913

Personnel records after this progressing date are closed to the public for seventy-five years. Only the person or his next of kin if deceased, can apply for details, and enquiries must be directed to:

Fleet Director, Naval Personnel
Disclosure Cell
Mail Point G2
Room 48
West Battery
Whale Island
Portsmouth
Hampshire
PO2 8DX

Ministry of Defence Medal Office
Entitlements to medals, and replacement of lost and stolen medals, are available only to the recipient or next of kin upon written request.

MOD Medal Office (MODMO) AFPPA
Building 250
RAF Innsworth
Gloucester
GL3 1HW

The Fleet Air Arm Museum Archive
The archive (see 4.5.2) is available to the public by prior arrangement. It is wise to check in advance that any Royal Marine service number sought is in the series held by the FAAM and is not among those held, for example, by the National Archives. However, because many documents can, at present, be accessed only by service number until a complete system of cross-indexing is in place, it is not always possible for the FAAM to provide a service number for a given name.

More information is given on the FAAM website: http://www.fleetairarm.com/pages/research/index.htm.
Those who wish to examine papers should contact:

Centre for Naval Aviation Records & Research
Fleet Air Arm Museum
Box D6, RNAS Yeovilton
Near Ilchester, Somerset
BA22 8HT
Tel: 01935 840565, selecting 2 for research.
Fax: 01935 842630
E-mail: research@fleetairarm.com

Imperial War Museum

When the Imperial War Museum was founded in 1917, one of its functions was to be a memorial to those who had died and suffered in the First World War. The museum has since expanded its remit to include all conflicts, concentrating on British and Commonwealth involvement from 1914 to the present day. The museum archives are held by the collecting departments and include personal letters, diaries, manuscripts, and unpublished memoirs, some of which relate to Royal Marines. There are in addition over 200 sound archive interviews of Royal Marines. Advice on how to use the archives to research family history is downloadable from their website.

Imperial War Museum
Lambeth Road
London
SE1 6HZ
Website: www.iwm.org.uk
E-mail: docs@iwm.org.uk

National Maritime Museum

The manuscripts section of the library of the National Maritime Museum holds both official and private records and papers relating to the royal and merchant navies, and maritime affairs generally.

The official papers include public records which complement series in the National Archives and the records of the Dreadnought Hospital, Greenwich. Private papers include business records, papers of individual naval officers and seamen, and artificial collections of naval historians and others.

For a detailed synopsis of the manuscript catalogue, refer to *A Guide to the Manuscripts in the National Maritime Museum* edited by R J B Knight (Mansell: 1977 & 1980). Volume 1 lists the personal collections, while volume 2 lists the public, business and artificial records.

4.4 Printed material and how to use it

The list of Further Reading towards the end of this work will detail secondary sources that will both provide the historical background of the Royal Marines and accounts of specific periods and units. The selection of titles that follows, with the description of their use, will give the researcher an idea of how to expand information gleaned from a basic record.

To identify ships or shore bases quoted in a service record, the following secondary sources can be used:

- *Ships of the Royal Navy*, J J Colledge (Greenhill 2003)
- *Shore Establishments of the Royal Navy*, B Warlow RN (Maritime Books 2000)

Having identified the ship or base, further details or operational history can be obtained by consulting a bibliography of Royal Navy ships and histories. There are many titles on specifically named ships, along with those giving histories of the types of ship. A standard Royal Navy history such as Laird Clowes's *A History of the Royal Navy* will cover operations and the ships involved, up to 1903. Beyond this date, the official histories of the war at sea in both world wars would be a fair start point. To identify and obtain details of Royal Marine units between 1914 and 1919, check the contents notes of Blumberg's *Britain's Sea Soldiers: The Royal Marines 1914–19*. For units between 1919 and 2000, see Appendix 4 of Ladd's *By Sea, By Land*. For identification and details of any medals either mentioned upon a service record, or visible in a photograph, the following sources will assist:

- *Ribbons & Medals*, H Taprell Dorling (Osprey 1983)
- *British Battles & Medals*, L L Gordon (Spink 1988)
- *Commando Gallantry Awards of WWII*, G A Brown (London Stamp Exchange 1991).

4.4.1 Navy, Army, and Marine Officer Lists
No original records of service of marine officers appointed before 1793 have survived; those after this date reside at the National Archives, Kew in the ADM 196 series, although those before around 1837 are incomplete. It is therefore useful, if researching a marine officer, to locate a run of Marine Officer Lists, the Navy List, and the Army List, as much can be extracted from a series of these to form a service history by way of appointments and promotions. By looking up the officer in question either by the index, or marine section in each issue, the progress of his career can be recorded. Once the name disappears from the index or retired list, it is a fair indication of the officer having left the service or having died. It is worth continuing onwards through the issues looking toward the rear of each volume, as removals from the list are sometimes explained, not always by an obituary notice.

The Marine Officers List did not appear in printed form before 1767 although the RM Museum has bound manuscript lists from 1760. Printed by the Admiralty annually, (although not always in the same month) they name all officers by descending rank in order of seniority and date of commission along with their assigned company number. Each volume usually contains a table of companies under the respective division, and will also indicate additional duties such as adjutant, quartermaster and so on. Before 1811 the index to each volume will list names alphabetically by seniority and rank. After that date the index changes to purely alphabetical order. In 1818 the format changed, and although a company table was included as before, the officer list merely gives an abbreviation of the division. The list continued in this form until being discontinued in 1886. The RM Museum Archive also holds a three-volume manuscript of marine officers' promotions compiled by a former military secretary Colonel Tom Hall RM in the late 1940s. The volumes (Arch 9/2/28) include all officers from 1755 to 1914.

The Army List was first printed annually in 1740. Before that, lists of regimental officers, including those of marine regiments, had been made since 1702. These lists are in the National Archive in WO 64, with a name index for those before 1754 on microfilm. The War Office produced the official monthly 'Army List' and the larger format annual 'List of Officers of the Army' simultaneously for a period, but from a marine's point of view the 1758 issue of the latter is useful as it lists the officers of marine regiments disbanded in 1748 and 1749, and then those of the new Corps in the same volume. Much of the remaining information contained in these lists is duplicated in the Marine or Navy Lists. From 1839 to 1915 a privately published Army List compiled by Lieutenant General H G Hart was produced containing details of officers' war services, which included Royal Marines. In 1954, the former half-yearly list that had become the 'Army Graduation List' began to include biographies, and Royal Marine officers of this period feature within it.

The Navy List, like the Army List, had both official and privately produced issues. *Steel's Original And Correct List of the Royal Navy & Hon. East India Company's Shipping* of 1782, predated the first official list produced by John Murray in 1814. However, the early issues are restricted to an active list of the Royal Navy's ships, and foreign captures, with later issues beginning to include naval officers by rank and commission. By 1799 marine officers are included along with their companies next to their names. This monthly list expands in both news and detail until in 1809, when the active list of ships at the front of each month gains a numbered column as they read alphabetically. This number is then repeated on the far right of an officer's name if he is aboard that ship. Other codes appear prefixed by the letter '*R*' and a number, and these are tabled at the end of the Royal Marines officers section as recruiting stations or districts. Early issues of *Steel's Navy List* also contain notice of courts martial, prize money awards and other miscellaneous items, along with, of course, a list of ships with their captains and number of guns and so forth.

The first Murray's list modifies this scheme by tabling the ship's officers in the numbered entry for the ship's name, and after a format change to a wider page width in 1846, an active naval officer index is added in April 1847. Royal Marines appeared in this index, with a numbered ship reference, in lists from July that year onwards.

The New Navy List appears in the 1830s compiled by Commander Charles Haultain KH RN. The early issues do not give biographical detail for Royal Marine officers due to an injunction brought against him by Lieutenant General Hart, and his Army List, but it at least gives up to five columns of data. These columns cover date of current commission and ship, along with date of joining the service, and any brevet rank attained (brevet rank was an award to an officer for distinguished service. He would be given a rank above that for which he was paid, thus giving him seniority in the Army List, but not in his regiment or Corps). By 1846 the dispute appears to have been resolved since brief Royal Marine officer biographies appear in *The New Navy List* although the title had been taken over by Joseph Allen Esq. RN, Greenwich Hospital.

In 1878, Lieutenant Colonel Francis Lean RMLI devised and published another quarterly Royal Navy List, expanding on Joseph Allen's approach to include biographical material and medal awards for both active and retired Naval and Royal Marines officers. This publication ran to the First World War when it was augmented with 'Who's Who in the Navy' prefaced by a history of the conduct of the war in the given year.

Although not a Navy List as such, mention should be made here of William O'Byrne's *A Naval Biographical Dictionary*. The first edition appeared in 1849, and followed similar biographical dictionaries of naval officers produced earlier by Charnock, Ralfe and Marshall between the 1790s and 1830s. The new and enlarged edition of O'Byrne of 1861 is of greater interest, as it contains Royal Marine officers' biographies. Unfortunately, only one volume was completed, which took the alphabetical surnames up to 'G'.

4.4.2 Official regulations

By the 1850s, selected regulations and instructions were printed towards the rear of each Navy List issue. These had begun with notification of medals such as the Naval General Service Medal of 1848 and the wearing of foreign orders. Navy Lists some twenty years later had added sections and tables showing pay rates, uniform regulations, entry and examination of officers, retirement, pensions, gratuities and allowances to widows and children and so on. Running parallel with this was the output of regulations from both parliament and the Admiralty, a selection of which is listed below. The Royal Marine genealogist will gain much detail of the rules and administration determining the service of a marine, as well as a description of their role and relationship with the naval service. The dates and ranges of issues to be found at the RM Museum Library are as follows:

- Sea Service Regulations 1790
- Regulations & Instructions for His Majesty's Service at Sea 1808
- Naval Regulations for Service at Sea 1825
- King's (Queen's) Regulations & Admiralty Instructions (1862–1987)
- Marine Mutiny Acts (1839–77)
- Marine Acts (raising and regulation whilst on shore/at sea) 1702–1877
- Royal Marines General Orders (1888–1936)
- General Standing Orders BR1253
- Royal Marines Instructions BR1283
- Royal Marines Routine Orders (RMROs)
- Promotions & Appointments Royal Marines (PARMs)

Official publications for internal use in the services were given a 'BR' number – BR1 was an ongoing list of all the titles designated. Between 1942 and 1951, BR1 listed over 2,000 official titles. Everything from the naval padre's Bible to the operating instructions for a galley fridge would have a BR number. Examples of relevance to the Royal Marine researcher would feature:

BR13 – bugler's handbook
BR81 – RN & RM uniform regulations
BR1006 – Royal Marine business 1944 (giving contemporary accounts of unit operations, training and tactics)
BR224 – gunnery pocket book
BR1736 – naval staff histories

The BR1736 series is very useful to the researcher as it offers naval operational histories of the Second World War, giving official accounts without the limitations of censorship, as they were restricted for internal use only. A good example relating to Royal Marines is Naval Staff History 429(1) and (2). This relates to 'Operation Neptune', the naval operations of D-Day 1944. While volume 1 gives a detailed narrative, volume 2 gives assembly points, convoy times and composition, escorts, landing craft with numbers or flotillas, craft lost or damaged and so on.

4.4.3 Official unit and general histories
The official repository for Royal Marines unit and war diaries is the National Archive, Kew. They are mainly to be found in the ADM 202 series and are currently open to the public to 1978. War diaries of the Royal Naval Division (1914–18) that include Royal Marines battalions can be found in the ADM 137 and WO 95 series.

The Royal Marines Museum archive contains commanders' unit diaries for

RM Commandos in the Arch 2/18/2–25 series. The maximum date range is 1943 to 1977, although not for every unit. Most fall within the 1950s to 1970s. The disbandment of 46, 47, and 48 RM Commandos after the Second World War prompted those units to produce privately published histories. The print run was primarily for their veterans as they paraded for the last time, so the books are now scarce. Originals are to be found in the RM Museum Library, and over the ensuing sixty-two years all the RM Commandos have had at least one book published on their history, with the exception of 42 Commando RM. The museum archive also has a large scrapbook compiled by the late Captain T G Linnell RM, covering documents and photographs he collected whilst serving in a heavy weapons troop of 7th RM Battalion, later reorganized as 48 RM Commando (Arch 11/14/18).

General Royal Marine histories and other titles appear in the Further Reading section of this book. To add to these, the chronology of Corps histories began with Captain Alexander Gillespie RM, who published the first account in 1803, followed in 1845 by Lieutenant Paul Harris Nicholas RM. His two-volume work drew heavily on the preceding title but added gazette letters from some of the operations. Richard Cannon produced a slim volume in his series of British regiments two years later, but it was Major Lourenço Edye RMLI who set the future standard of detailed research with his *Historical Records of the Royal Marines–Volume 1, 1664-1701* (1893). Unfortunately, the manuscript of volume two was a victim of imperial Germany's unrestricted U-boat warfare in 1917, while on passage to Britain from South America! Much of Edye's research notes (Arch 11/12/30–32) were used by Colonel Cyril Field RMLI and General Sir H E Blumberg KCB RM, who between them produced three volumes entitled *Britain's Sea Soldiers*. Field produced the first two in 1924, which took the history from 1664 to 1913, while Blumberg published the third in 1927, covering 1914–1919. Quite apart from these works, the two authors produced other research both commercially and via the offices of the *Globe & Laurel* such as *History of the Royal Marine Divisions* in 1931 (with contributions from Captains Grover, Thomas and Major Congdon) and *Random Records* (1935). With Fraser and Carr-Laughton's *The Royal Marine Artillery* having been published in 1930, the Royal Marines had, in effect, reviewed and updated their history in a productive nine years.

In 1979 a former HO temporary Lieutenant James Landon RM, completed a manuscript that would progress the story of the Royal Marines from 1919 to 1980. Under the *nom de plume* James D Ladd, this book was printed again, after revision and updating, in 1998 as *By Sea, By Land* and remains the standard reference for this period.

4.4.4 RM periodicals, magazines and newspapers

The major reference source of use to Royal Marines genealogists and historians alike is the Corps journal the *Globe & Laurel*, named after the regimental insignia of the Royal Marines. The first issue was published on 1 May 1892, for private circulation at 1d a month. It was sold in all messes and divisional canteens, and apart from current Corps news, it contained promotions and appointments. These sections grew in size with the latter forming a 'gazette' within each issue. Embarkations and disembarkations were added, along with sport and correspondence, births, deaths and marriages. The obituaries in the early issues tend to be for officers or long serving non-commissioned officers, with just a column entry of dates of death for other ranks and pensioners. It is not until the 1980s editions that other ranks begin to have biographical obituaries. During the world wars and other conflicts, casualties and prisoners of war would be listed, along with notifications of honours and awards. Outside the war years, sport features prominently, with team and individual achievements often recorded in detail, sometimes with photographs. Reports are also received from the fleet and foreign stations with named recipients of shooting medals, rowing cups and trophies and boxing competitions. Many a 'face to a name' has been discovered in a 1920s tug-of-war team photograph.

It is worth noting that the issues up to First World War also contain retrospective historical articles including two recurring features, 'A Century Ago' and 'Corps News from the Sixties' (1860s). Both of these were compiled by Major Lourenço Edye RMLI, the contemporary historian of the Royal Marines and future editor of the magazine. A retrospective index has recently been compiled, while card indexes of RM officers and RM Band ranks are contained in the RM Museum Library. The magazine continues to be published to this day with an issue every two months.

The RN School of Music and the RM Band service launched the first issue of their magazine, *The Blue Band*, in December 1949, to be printed three times a year. The magazine covered the activities of the bands and matters affecting them, along with information on bandmasters and obituaries. As of yet, there is no overall index to the journal, although individual issues do have a contents page.

At various times, individual Royal Marines units and ships' detachments have produced their own newspapers and magazines, some being more unofficial than others, but much detail can be gleaned from these publications for the Royal Marine researcher. A sample of some of the publications is listed below to give an idea of the scope of the periods and units covered.

The 3rd Jungle Book, nine issues relating to 3rd Special Service Brigade in Burma and the Arakan, April 1944 to March 1946

The Jungle Journal, a unit-produced newspaper of 42 Commando RM in Malaya *c.* 1951–2

Four-Two, a unit-produced magazine of 42 Commando RM between 1960 and 1964, covering deployments to Brunei, Sarawak, Borneo and Aden

XL, a unit-produced magazine of 40 Commando RM during the 1979–80 tour of duty in Northern Ireland

Armagh Nights, a unit-produced magazine of 41 Commando RM during the 1980 deployment to Armagh, Northern Ireland

Splash, a ship-produced newspaper of Landing Craft Flak 42 in 1944. The vessel served at both D-Day and the assault upon Walcheren

Buzz, the magazine of HMS *Royal Harold* 1946–7. This was actually NP1742 based at Kiel after the Second World War to secure and oversee repair of the port and canal

Tiger Times (incorporating *Desert Despatch*): this unit-produced newspaper of 45 Commando RM followed their deployments between Malta and Malaya between 1950 and 1953

Commando News was a news-sheet produced for 3 Commando Brigade *c.* 1951

Lympstone Bugle, the newspaper of the Commando Training Centre RM *c.* 1971–5

In addition to these titles, the RM Commando units would produce their own newsletters, and examples of these are held in the RM Museum archive:

Arch 2/18/3, 40 Commando RM newsletters 1961–78
Arch 2/18/4, 41 Commando RM newsletters 1961–77
Arch 2/18/5, 42 Commando RM newsletters 1961–5
Arch 2/18/6, 43 Commando RM newsletters 1961–8
Arch 2/18/8, 45 Commando RM newsletters 1960–78
Arch 2/18/14, Commando Logistic Regiment newsletters 1973–8
Arch 2/18/30, 3 Commando Brigade Air Squadron newsletters 1974–7

4.4.5 Other periodicals, magazines and newspapers

Commercially produced contemporary newspapers are an obvious source for information of events that may feature in the research of a Royal Marine ancestor. Locally produced papers in the port locations of Chatham, Plymouth, Portsmouth, Woolwich and Deal should be checked first, though in the nineteenth century titles such as *The Times*, the *London Gazette*, *Morning Advertiser*, *Daily News* and the *Pall Mall Gazette* printed official letters of actions, from the despatches received by the Admiralty. These would often include named casualties. Papers like *The Times* and the *Hampshire Telegraph* also have constructed indexes. The repository for national and local newspapers and their records is:

The British Newspaper Library
Colindale Avenue
London
NW9 5HE
Tel: 020 7412 7353
Fax: 020 7412 7379
E-mail: newspaper@bl.uk

The following papers and journals are a selection of titles in which useful contemporary or researched material can be found:

Navy News, 1954 to date (Also available on a CD-ROM with an archive online)
The Fleet, 1905–18
Ashore & Afloat, 1899–1967
Mariners Mirror, 1911 to date
Army Historical Research Society, 1921 to date
Military Historical Society, 1965 to date
Band International, 1978 to date (newsletters from *c.* 1974)
Navy Review, 1914 to date
Navy & Army Illustrated, 1895 to 1914 (1st series)
Naval Chronicle, 1799–1818
Military Chronicle, 1810–12
Royal Military Panorama, 1812–14
London Illustrated News, to date
London Gazette, 1665 to date
Journal of the Orders Medals Research Society, 1966 to date
The *Sheet Anchor*, the journal of the RM Historical Society 1968 to date

4.4.6 Memoirs and secondary accounts

While a personal diary possesses immediacy, a journal or memoir suggests a leisurely, more deliberate approach to recording a historical experience. Each has their value for the researcher. A bibliography of Royal Marine titles will feature many biographies and autobiographies of former officers and men. With the ease of computer desktop publishing, the amateur author can be encouraged to assemble his thoughts for his or his family's amusement. It is no longer a prerequisite to be famous, or to have done something worthy to write or be written about.

The self-produced pamphlet or booklet can contain unique material about a place or little-known event amongst the personal story, and this can be valuable to the researcher as long as they are able to know of its existence. The Internet can be of great use for finding notice of these works, for example, by just entering into a search engine the name of a place where it is known the ancestor served.

Other accounts that can be of interest are produced by veterans' associations via their newsletters or publications. The *Newfoundland Times* is produced by former crew members of the cruiser HMS *Newfoundland,* and includes articles from the association's members about her history in the Second World War and postwar operations such as Suez in 1956. The Landing Craft Gun & Flak Association canvassed its members to fill in a questionnaire giving details of the craft they served on and the activities they remembered. The two archive boxes of replies are now in the RM Museum Archive (Arch 14/18/9–13).

The bibliography downloadable from the RM Museum website at www.royalmarinesmuseum.co.uk will give the researcher a good idea of what is available.

4.5 Register and service numbers

The practice of allocating register numbers to ranks was officially instituted on 1 July 1885. The Admiralty ordered 'that every person belonging to the Royal Marines, except Commissioned Officers, shall be described by a Register Number in conjunction with Letters indicating the Divisions to which he belongs, instead of his Company and Division as heretofore', and that the suffixes 'RMA' and 'RMLI' should be used whenever sufficient from a legal point of view.

The four divisions had begun to allocate register numbers long before; Chatham began in 1842, Portsmouth in 1843, Plymouth in 1856 and the Royal Marine Artillery in 1859. There is evidence to suggest that the description books were kept concurrently, and it is quite possible that a man entered at, say, Plymouth Division between 1856 and 1885, and was allocated an 'old style' number rather than a register number. The official institution of register numbers in 1885 may have been an attempt to regulate the administrative muddle that resulted. It was suggested that each division keep a General Register of Service Numbers Index. This was taken up, and these eventually formed the vast part of ADM 313 at TNA, Kew.

The letters indicating the division to which a rank belonged became 'CH' indicating Chatham Division Royal Marine Light Infantry, 'PLY' indicating Plymouth Division Royal Marine Light Infantry, 'PO' indicating Portsmouth Division Royal Marine Light Infantry, and 'RMA' indicating Royal Marine

Artillery. The Royal Marine Artillery and Royal Marine Light Infantry were amalgamated on 22 June 1923 and the prefix 'RMA' was dropped. The prefixes 'CH', 'PLY', and 'PO' were retained though to indicate the locations of the three remaining divisions, now styled 'Royal Marines'. The suffixes 'RMA' and 'RMLI' were dropped at the same time, and 'RM' was substituted.

The register number allocated to a rank entered at one of the divisions after the amalgamation simply followed on from the last number allocated before 22 June 1923; for example, after CH12346 George Smith RMLI came CH12347 William Brown RM. All numbers of up to five figures which follow the prefixes 'CH', 'PLY' or 'PO' indicated ranks entered in the Royal Marine Light Infantry (and subsequently Royal Marines) divisions before October 1925. All numbers of up to five figures which follow the prefix 'RMA' indicate ranks entered in the Royal Marine Artillery before the amalgamation. Any Royal Marine Artillery man who then transferred to the new Portsmouth Division, retained his old number but substituted his 'RMA' prefix with 'PO'. To prevent any duplication of numbers with the former Portsmouth RMLI division, a number '2' was added ahead of his old number, so RMA17654 Frederick Jones RMA became PO 217654 Frederick Jones RM.

The suffixes 'N' or 'S' to any of the 'CH', 'PLY', 'PO' or 'RMA' numbers indicate a rank who entered one of these divisions for short service during the First World War; for example, PLY 13756S John Williams RMLI. The prefix 'RMB' followed by the number of up to four figures indicated a rank entered at the Royal Naval School of Music between its foundation in 1903 and before October 1925. The prefix 'D' followed by a number of up to three figures indicates a rank entered on the permanent establishment of the Depot, Royal Marines Deal, between 1866 and February 1947. This practice was discontinued, and the ranks transferred to Chatham, Plymouth or Portsmouth and allocated the next available register numbers. The same prefix, followed by a number of up to four figures and the suffixes 'N' or 'S', indicates a rank entered in the Royal Marine Divisional Engineers, the Royal Marine Divisional Train, the Royal Marine Medical Unit, the Royal Marine Ordnance Company or the Royal Marine Labour Corps for short service during the First World War.

In October 1925, the letter 'X' was added to the prefixes to indicate 'men enlisted and re-entered in the . . . Royal Marines under the revised rates of pay . . . i.e. entries and re-entries on and after 5 October 1925, except re-entries before 2 November 1925, after a break in service of less than five years', and a new sequence of numbers, beginning at 1, was started in each register. By the time this practice was superseded in the Chatham, Plymouth and Portsmouth registers in 1948, these sequences had reached four figures. The Royal Marine Band Service continued to use the 'X' until August 1955 though, and then the old sequence of numbers was resumed, but at 3,400 above the last number allocated before October 1925 to prevent any duplication.

The prefixes 'CH/X', 'PLY/X', 'PO/X' and 'RMB/X' followed by numbers of six figures in the 100,000 series, indicate ranks entered for short service during the Second World War. The prefix 'EX' followed by a number of three or four figures, indicated a special Reservist entered at Exton Division between October 1939 and July 1940. The ranks holding these numbers were then transferred to Chatham, Plymouth or Portsmouth and allocated a number in the six-figure series. The prefix 'RM', followed by a number of four or five figures was adopted in 1948 and superseded the Chatham, Plymouth and Portsmouth ones. It indicated a rank entered on a continuous or short service engagement between January 1948 and January 1973. The same prefix, followed by a number of six figures, indicated a national serviceman entered between January 1948 and June 1952.

A prefix 'RME', followed by a number of three or four figures and the suffix 'S' indicated a rank of the Royal Marine Engineers entered for short service during the First World War. This should not be confused with the Royal Marine Divisional Engineers of the Royal Naval Division, who were allocated numbers with a 'D' prefix. The 'RME' prefix, followed by a number of five figures, indicates a rank of the Royal Marine Engineers of the Second World War. The prefix 'AUX', followed by a number of up to four figures, indicated a member of the Auxiliary Battalion formed during the Second World War. Subsequently, these ranks were transferred to Plymouth and allocated numbers in the six-figure sequence.

In 1952 the Admiralty decided to institute a system to indicate whether or not a Reservist was a national serviceman. The prefix 'RMV' followed by a five-figure number indicated that a man became a Reservist either prior to the establishment of national service or after his national service. The prefix 'RM(V)9', followed by a five-figure number, indicated that a man was a Reservist during whole-time national service. The prefix 'RM V 9', followed by a five-figure number, indicated that a man was a Reservist during part-time national service. On 1 July 1955, all but one of these prefixes ('RMV'), were abolished, and all Reservists, whether serving on or discharged before that date, were allocated a new number with the 'RMV' prefix. To prevent duplication, this new series had six figures beginning at 200,000.

On 1 February 1973, all prefixes in use were replaced and 'CH/X' became 'POO', 'PLY/X' became 'SOO', 'PO/X' became 'ROO' and 'RM' became 'PO'. 1973 saw the introduction of computerized service numbers for officers and ratings; prior to this RN and RM officers did not have service numbers. RM officers' computer numbers started with the letter 'N', and other ranks with the letter 'P'. On 1 November 2006 under Joint Personnel Administration (harmonization and simplification of all Human Resources administration processes) all service numbers for new joiners started with the digit 3 followed by seven further digits.

4.5.1 Individual service documents

The three principal documents that the Royal Marines genealogist would either have or would be seeking are the Attestation, Certificate of Service, and Certificate of Discharge. They represent the enlistment, activity and disposal of a marine, and record the identity, and to a lesser or greater degree, details of a man 'being' a Royal Marine.

The Attestation (R165)

The attestation document would consist of a number of formal questions (depending on slight alterations and revisions to R165 at various times) with answers eventually sworn under oath in front of a magistrate (or attesting officer) within four days of enlisting. Prior to that, the potential recruit was 'served notice', which was originally a separate document, but later appears printed on the reverse of a 'copy' of attestation given to the man at enlistment. Apart from name, address, age and marital status, typical other questions would be about trade or work, imprisonment, fitness and disorders, previous military service, and on later versions what length of term of service was being signed to. Specimen attestations from the 1840s also ask the amount of bounty received. When attested, the recruit would be read the 3rd, 4th and 5th Articles of War as they would appear in the Marine Mutiny Act at the time. These would inform him that cowardice and treachery, failure or delay in obeying orders, mutiny and sedition, and desertion in action would be punishable by death. Negligence of duty would result in dismissal.

The Certificate of Service (R138)

The researcher will probably be faced with two forms of service record, the S1241 or R138 Certificate of Service and the Register of Service entry from the ADM 159 series at the National Archives. The former is the document that the Royal Marine himself would have been issued at the time of his discharge; the latter is usually copied from the Registers of Service at Kew, either from the original or a microfilm. Both contain similar, if not identical, information. The R138 is a four-sided folded foolscap vellum, parchment, linen-backed or paper document depending on the period. The register document containing all the details would usually be on a single ledger side.

The front page of the certificate, after giving the name, will state the first division on enlistment on the left and the register or service number on the right. Below this will be found date of birth and origin, trade and religion. To

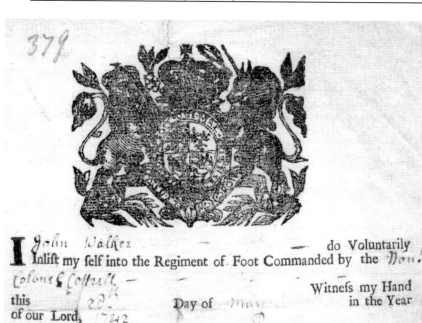

379

I *John Walker* do Voluntarily
Inlift my felf into the Regiment of. Foot Commanded by the *Hon.*
Colonel Cottrell —
this *28* Day of *May* Witnefs my Hand
of our Lord, *1742* in the Year

County of
Stafford

Thefe are to Certify; That the abovefaid *John Walker*
Aged *26.* Years of the Parifh of *Wolverhampton* in the County of
Stafford a *lockfmith* by Trade Came before me, one of his Majefty's Juftices
of the Peace and acknowledged to have fairly and Voluntarily Inlifted
himfelf to ferve his Majefty King G E O R G E in the abovefaid Regiment; and took the Oath of Fidelity to his Majefty, and had the Articles of War Relating to Mutiny and Defertion, read to him: In Witnefs
hereof, I here Set my Han d this *28* Day of *May* in
the Year of our Lord *1742*

*An early attestation paper of John Walker, 1742. He was unusual in that he could
obviously read and write.*

140

the right will be the name and address of the next of kin, below which will be a basic description of the man. Service qualifications are next recorded on the left, with school certificates on the right, with a 'yes or no' swimming question answered underneath. The last two boxes record employment during service, and medals issued.

On opening the certificate the column format spreads across the open length, and here will be listed the man's rank, company, division or ship, number on ship's book, date of entry and discharge from that ship or division, cause (which usually shows embarked, disembarked, or headquarters), and a character rating of fair/good/very good. 'Ability' is the next column, marked 'Sat.'(satisfactory), Good, or V.G. The 'recommended for medal and gratuity' column does not tend to be filled in until the bottom of the sheet, if at all. Each line is then signed off by the commandant of the division, or ship's captain.

The back page consists of services forfeited, conduct and badges, promotions and reductions, and payments for wounds and hurts, prize money and other gratuities. Services forfeited will often show a man having served underage. On discovery, the period up to the minimum entry age will be forfeited against engagement, conduct badges and pension. In other words, the man would have to serve that element of time again. It is important to consider that all the elements recorded link together, and the checking of dates of punishments should relate to a fall in the mark of the conduct column aboard a ship listed within that date, for example. Many of the abbreviated entries will be found in Appendix 2 of this book.

The Discharge Certificate (R111)
By 1918 this document had received a number of revisions and standardizations that enabled it to be filled in as a form. Much of the detail was extracted from the certificate of service with the addition of the calculations of his entitled reckonable time in years, months and days towards pay and pension. The reverse of the certificate would give a physical description of the man and an intended address of residence. A blank area was provided headed 'Engagements' and 'Wounds' that may or may not be filled in with ships and actions; this seems to vary from document to document. The final box was provided to record any 'Marching Money' or travel warrant monies issued for the man to return home.

Specimen versions of this certificate from the 1840s, where they exist, tend to be written in greater detail than later ones, and include a conduct testimonial, and a breakdown of time spent at sea opposed to time spent ashore. Sometimes the names of ships served in are given, as well as an analysis of time of service at any given rank if promoted during the term. This can make this document important to the researcher where a certificate of service is not available for the man in question.

4.5.2 Group records

Records of the Royal Marines at the National Archives
Service records of the Royal Marines currently up to 1928 are held at the National Archives. Royal Marine officers' records are definitive from 1837 and are on microfilm (ADM 196 Series), with an index available on the shelves. A full page of A3 gives varying detail about the origins of each officer and of his active career. The later records become progressively more detailed, although poor condition or photography – or both – can make them difficult to read. The use of this record group can save the time taken to construct a career piecemeal from the Army and Navy Lists, or the Marine Officers Lists (Seniority List of Officers of the [Royal] Marines from 1757 to 1886) as described in 4.4.1. If need be, the latter mentioned lists can be found in both ADM 118/230–336 (1757 to 1850, indexed from 1770), and in ADM 192/1–44 (1760 to 1886). The Royal Marines Museum Library also has a bound set of these.

ADM 313/110 is an index to the records of service residing in ADM 196/58–65, ADM 196/83 and ADM 196/97–105. A copy is also available in the Microfilm Reading Room. ADM 196/106–116 contains officer service records for entry into the Royal Marines between 1884 and 1923, all of which have integral indexes. Records of Royal Marine Artillery officers for the years 1804 to 1855 (and in some cases serving until 1870) are in ADM 196/66, and an indexed list of Royal Marine warrant officers appointed between 1904 and 1912 (and serving up to 1923) is in ADM 196/67.

It is worth noting that the ADM 96 series (records of the [Royal] Marines Pay Office) lists officers on half-pay at particular times including the reduction of the Corps on the conclusion of the peace between Britain and France in 1814. Some documents abbreviate this to 'ROPE' (reduced on peace establishment). This document is useful in that it gives the officers' addresses. ADM 96 pieces 155 to 365 cover the period of the Revolutionary and Napoleonic Wars (1790–1815) and are also useful for records of other ranks in this period. It consists mainly of 'Effective & Subsistence Lists'. These were the shore company muster lists for the marines, and include men subsisted by other divisions. They are relatively complete from 1796 onwards. All the pieces follow in year sequence except -7268 (1806, 58th–69th Companies) found amongst the year 1807, and -7307 (1805, 63rd–105th Companies) located in the year 1811. Piece 366, covering the year 1816 should be included, as it contains information on the colonial marines who served from 1814 against the Americans.

A description of records of non-commissioned officers and men is listed below, in two groups. The first group includes the records that relate directly to the service of non-commissioned men, and the second to records that might contain references to them or their dependants. Records of the births, marriages and deaths of marines' wives and children were kept separately by each division and are included in group 'A' below. Also given are the National Archives reference numbers against the description of these documents.

A detailed list of all relevant entries is beyond the capacity of this book, so a visit to their website (www.nationalarchives.gov.uk) to check online catalogues and sources, including their Military Records Information sheets 45, 47 and 48, is worthwhile.

A note on the records described as Group A
The rotational company numbering system has been previously mentioned (see 1.2.2) and the periodic variation in the number borne on the strength of the Corps, and the number of divisions, reflected the international situation. During the American War of Independence (1775–83), for instance, the number of companies rose to 157, but was reduced to 70 at the peace of 1783. In 1805 a new division, at Woolwich, was established to supply additional companies committed to the Napoleonic War. Royal Marine Artillery companies were raised at each of these divisions from 1804, eventually being established as a separate entity in 1859. This can be viewed on the illustration of company tables on page 10.

The divisions maintained the responsibility for keeping the records for their non-commissioned ranks until after the Second World War, so the list of records, that follow, has been divided into divisions. The earliest type of record of service appears in the description books. In 1885, these were super-seded by the Registers of Service when the Admiralty ordered 'that every person belonging to Royal Marines, except commissioned officers, shall be described by a Register Number in conjunction with letters indicating the Division to which he belongs, instead of his Company, and Division as hereto-fore'. The letters indicating the division were 'CH' to represent Chatham, 'PLY' to represent Plymouth, 'PO' to represent Portsmouth, and 'RMA' to represent the Royal Marine Artillery. As we have seen (section 4.5), all four of them had, in fact, started to allocate register numbers to their recruits long before, so the record of service of a man who enlisted, for example, into Plymouth Division between 1856 and 1885 might be found in either the description books or in the Registers of Service.

According to a file within the Royal Marine Office papers for 1885 (ADM 1/6796), the idea of the Registers of Service was first aired in a circular dated 24 December 1884 from the Deputy Adjutant General, RM and they officially came into use from the start of the September quarter of 1885 on 24 June that year, although the register numbers appear to have been issued for all men from 1 January 1885. It appears to have been introduced as an economy measure to help centralize information as the following quote from the original circular shows:

> The different particulars of a Marine's services which are now recorded in various separate books will be brought together in this Central Register, and when the system is fairly established will render the use of the 'General Description Book' (R23), as well as the 'Size Book for Recruits' (R20), the Adjutants Effective List (R2), the Embarkation and Disembarkation Books (R3 & R7) and Drill Register (R31), no longer necessary.
>
> The record of each Man's services to be indicated by a Register number, and with a view to uniformity at each Division as well as to ensure that the numbers shall be arranged approximately according to length of service, it is suggested that the numbering should commence with the oldest soldiers whose names appear in the Description Book under letter A, for a period say of 5 years, that it be then continued to those recorded to letter B for the same period, and this course pursued until all the letters of the alphabet have been so dealt with. The next oldest portion of the Division should then be taken in like manner through the alphabet, and then the next, until the numbering has been completed, the periods taken being longer or shorter as may be considered most convenient and practicable.
>
> This numbering of the Division should be proceeded with at once, in existing Description Books, so that the work of transcription may be facilitated and the numbers to be given to men newly joined from 1st January [1885] fixed.
>
> By the adoption of this Register the preparation of duplicate Parchment certificates for every man will no longer be necessary, the duplicate certificates already prepared may be retained but no further entries need to be made on them unless called for.

A chronological/alphabetical index by division (ADM 313 Series) can be searched to find the man's number, armed with which it is possible to access the appropriate volume or reel of microfilm. The man's record occupies a full page of A3 and contains detailed information of his origins, physical attributes, movements, courses and assessments. A note on his operational experiences is sometimes on the bottom right-hand corner, where, unfortunately, greasy thumbs and poor photography often make it difficult to read. If this is the case, ask to see the original from the repository, although be prepared for the process to take a week or two.

Before a search of these records can be started, it is necessary to discover the division to which the subject of the research belonged, if it is not already known. Sometimes this can be found by reading the muster rolls of HM ships for a particular year, if it is known he was serving in a certain ship at a certain time; or the rolls of Royal Marines recipients of a certain campaign medal, if it is known he received one. These records are also held at the National Archives. It may help the researcher to remember that, prior to 1947 ships' detachments were usually drawn from the same RM divisions as the 'home' port of the ship. If none of this information is to hand, the place of the man's marriage and death might provide a starting point. For instance, a man who married a woman from Devon or Cornwall might be a Plymouth 'rank', and a man who died in Hampshire or Sussex might be a Portsmouth one. If the researcher does not have this detail either, a search of the attestation or discharge records for each of the divisions may be necessary starting with the year when it is thought the subject enlisted, or was discharged from, the Royal Marines.

Group A

Description:	TNA Reference
1. Chatham Division	
Attestations, 1790–1883	ADM 157/1–139
Description books, 1755–1884	ADM 158/1–32
Registers of service, 1842–1905	ADM 159/36–60
General weekly returns, 1755–1869	ADM 183/42–98
Embarkation book, 1878–84	ADM 183/99
Muster rolls of HM ships, 1883	ADM 183/100
Discharge books, 1773–1884	ADM 183/101–110
Disposal books, 1814–86	ADM 183/111–113
Registers of marriages, 1865–84	ADM 183/114–115
Registers of marriages & births of children, 1830–84	ADM 183/116–117
Registers of marriages and births & deaths of children, 1862–1913	ADM 183/118–119
Historical notes and extracts relating to the Royal Marines at Chatham, 1761–1827	ADM 201/50

Description:	TNA Reference
2. Depot RM, Deal	
Disposal books 1874–82 (see also Group 7 below)	ADM 193/1–2
3. Plymouth Division	
Attestations, 1804–38	ADM 157/140
Attestations and discharges, 1842–83	ADM 157/141–337
Description books, c. 1763–1884	ADM 158/207–283
Registers of Service, 1856–1902	ADM 159/61–79
General weekly returns, 1761–1919	ADM 184/24–34
Embarkation books, 1803–09 and 1819–32	ADM 184/36–37
Discharge book, 1784–1892	ADM 184/38–41
Disposal book, 1788–97	ADM 184/42
Registers of marriages and births & deaths of children, 1862–1920	ADM 184/43–54
4. Portsmouth Division	
Attestations, 1804–36	ADM 157/338–352
Attestations and discharges, 1837–83	ADM 157/353–615
Description books, 1796–1888	ADM 158/91–206
Registers of service, 1843–1901	ADM 159/1–19
General weekly returns, 1797–1820	ADM 185/38–61
Embarkation book, 1803–14	ADM 185/62
Discharge books, 1816–88	ADM 185/63–67
Disposal book, 1874–7	ADM 185/68
Register of marriages, 1869–81	ADM 185/69
5. Royal Marine Artillery	
Description books, ?–1848	ADM 158/77–85
Description books, ?–1884	ADM 158/86–90
Registers of service, 1859–1901	ADM 159/20–35

Description:	TNA Reference
Embarkation books, 1805–37	ADM 193/7
Disposal book, 1845–59	ADM 193/8
Register of marriages and baptisms, 1810–53 (see also Group 7 below)	ADM 193/9

6. Woolwich Division

List of personnel of the division, 1806–22	ADM 6/407
General weekly returns, 1868–9	ADM 81/10
Embarkation books, 1805–14	ADM 81/11
Discharge book, 1806–69	ADM 81/12–22
Marriage roll, 1822–53	ADM 81/23
Register of marriages, 1852–69	ADM 81/24
Register of baptisms, 1824–68	ADM 81/25
Description books, 1805–68 (see also Group 7 below)	ADM 158/33–76

7. Miscellaneous Records

Lists of Royal Marines who purchased their discharges, 1818–24	ADM 6/408
Sheerness RM Church baptisms, 1866–1921	ADM 6/437
Seniority lists of warrant officers, 1832–44	ADM 118/212–229
Miscellaneous attestations, 1869–83	ADM 157/616–659
Miscellaneous discharge certificates, 1761–1843	ADM 193/18

[The attestation and discharge certificates in this group may contain those for the Depot, the Royal Marine Artillery and Woolwich Division]

Group B

Description	TNA Reference
1. Pensions and Allowances	
Miscellaneous papers relating to the proceedings of the commissioner for managing the charity for the relief of widows, 1816–30	ADM 6/389–402
Miscellaneous papers and correspondence on discharges, pensions, pay and compensation, 1806–78	ADM 201/20
Good Conduct Medals and Gratuities, 1849–84	ADM 201/21
Greenwich Hospital Pensions, 1862–1908	ADM 201/22–23
2. Order Books of the Division	
Chatham	
Order books, 1767–1941	ADM 183/1–37
Plymouth	
Order books, 1760–1881	ADM 184/1–14
Commanding officer's order books, 1833–36	ADM 184/15–16
Pembroke Dock divisional order books, 1845–50	ADM 184/17–18
Garrison order book, 1873	ADM 184/199
Portsmouth	
Garrison and divisional order books, 1806–1941	ADM 185/1–33
Royal Marine Artillery	
Order books, 1890–1918	ADM 193/2–6
3. Correspondence to and from the Divisions	
Chatham	
Adjutant General RMs letter book – to Chatham, 1869–84	ADM 58/1–21
Admiralty letters – to Chatham, 1755–1826	ADM 183/121–125
Letter books – from Chatham, 1823–84	ADM 183/126–129
Depot, RM Deal	
Adjutant General RMs letter books – to Deal, 1868–84	ADM 62/1–18

Description	TNA Reference
Plymouth	
Adjutant General RMs letter books – to Plymouth, 1868–84	ADM 61/1–17
Portsmouth	
Letter books – from Portsmouth, 1772–1853	ADM 185/71–79
Miscellaneous letters from Portsmouth, 1816–1922 and 1899–1906	ADM 185/80–81
Letter books – to the Admiralty, 1789–1817	ADM 185/82–104
Letters from the RM Barracks at Portsmouth and Gosport to the RM Office, 1833–70	ADM 201–2
Royal Marine Artillery	
Adjutant General RMs letter books – to the Royal Marine Artillery, 1868–84	ADM 59/1–17
RM Office – correspondence and papers relating to the Royal Marine Artillery, 1804–73	ADM 201/31
Woolwich	
Adjutant General RMs letter books – to Woolwich, 1868–9	ADM 57/1–2
Letter books etc. covering all divisions	
Adjutant General RMs divisional letter books, 1806–67	ADM 56/1–107
Adjutant General RMs divisional letter books, 1871–84	ADM 63/1–12
RM Office – letter book containing correspondence with the War Office and the RM Divisions, 1868–9	ADM 200/1
RM Office – brigade order book; correspondence with the commandants of divisions and 'in-letters' from the divisions, 1831–8	ADM 201/1

4. Correspondence between the RM Office and the Admiralty

Entry books – letters to the Admiralty, 1826–68	ADM 191/1–37
Entry books – minutes to the Admiralty, 1862–8	ADM 191/28–32
Entry books – letters and minutes to the Admiralty, 1868–9	ADM 191/33–34

Description	TNA Reference
Entry books – submissions to the Secretary of the Admiralty, 1869–75	ADM 191/35–39
Letters from Inspector General RM, mostly to the Admiralty, 1860–68	ADM 201/3
Inspector General RMs reports and minutes to the Admiralty, 1862–8	ADM 201/5
Numbers: all ranks of Royal Marines available for mobilization, 1898	ADM 201/52
Return of numbers entered, discharged, deserted, etc., 1899–1900	ADM 201/53
Returns to the Admiralty, 1869–81	ADM 201/70
Returns of numbers of officers, warrant and non-commissioned officers, and men, ashore and afloat, 1884–98	ADM 201/71

5. Financial and Educational Matters

Savings bank and stationery allowance, 1825–68	ADM 201/33
Savings bank, 1843–67	ADM 201/34–36
Schools and teachers, 1840–90	ADM 201/37
Returns showing the financial prospects of a non-commissioned officer from enlistment to discharge, 1898	ADM 201/51

6. Royal Marine Units Serving Overseas

South Africa Battalion – order book, 1879	ADM 163/38
Ireland Battalion – order book, 1880–1	ADM 183/39
Special Battalion of the Royal Marine Light Infantry, formed for service in the Mediterranean: quartermaster's diary, 1882	ADM 185/70
1st Brigade – Canton, China: memoranda book, 1858–60	ADM 193/11
1st Battalion, Royal Marine Light Infantry – Canton, China: list of promotions and letter book, 1859	ADM 193/12

Description	TNA Reference
South Africa Battalion: muster roll, 1879	ADM 193/13
South Africa Battalion: letter book, 1879	ADM 193/14
2nd Battalion Suez: order book, 1884–85	ADM 193/15
Royal Marine Light Infantry Battalion, Suakin and Sudan: order book, 1885	ADM 193/16
Papers from overseas posts, 1809–78	ADM 201/38
Ashanti, 1873–4	ADM 201/39
China, 1840–1902	ADM 201/40–43
Esquimalt, 1883–96	ADM 201/44
Japan, 1862–75	ADM 201/45
Suakin, 1884–5	ADM 201/46–49

7. Courts Martial Register

Description	TNA Reference
Chatham Division, 1902–05	ADM 194/1
Portsmouth Division, 1834–1916	ADM 194/2–17
Portsmouth Division – Royal Marines Detachments in HM ships, 1836–9 and 1859–74	ADM 194/18–19
Plymouth Division: north coast of Spain Battalion, 1836–45	ADM 194/20
Plymouth Division, 1845–98	ADM 194/21–32
Plymouth Division: district courts martial, 1898–1902	ADM 194/33
Plymouth Division: district and regimental courts martial, 1902–14	ADM 194/34–38
Royal Marine China Battalion: Chatham, Woolwich and 1st Battalion ranks, 1857–60	ADM 194/39
Woolwich and 2nd Battalion Royal Marine Light Infantry, 1857–60	ADM 194/40
Royal Marine Japan Battalion, 1864–65	ADM 194/41
Royal Navy officers and ratings and Royal Marines, 1812–55	ADM 194/42

Description	TNA Reference
Royal Navy officers 1857–1915 (these may include Royal Marine officers)	ADM 194/43–45

[N.B.: courts martial registers are closed for seventy-five years after the last court martial in the piece]

Medal rolls

Admiralty medal rolls and medal lists are held in the ADM 171 series, and are also contained on microfilm alphabetically by ship or RM unit. If the researcher has a reference that their subject was present at an action where a medal was awarded, this source can be a comparatively simple route into the paper trail of records. It is worth noting that many medal rolls have been researched and published commercially, and so you can save time by checking library catalogues.

Coastguard service, 1900–23

Sometimes Royal Marines who had completed a term of service and had not registered for the RFR (Royal Fleet Reserve) or had been discharged due to age or condition of fitness found employment in the coastguard service. Service record cards of Royal Marines (and Naval Ratings), 1900–23, are arranged alphabetically in ADM 175/82A to ADM 175/84B, and for Royal Marines alone, 1919–23, in ADM 175/90.

Casualties: general

The registers of killed and wounded in ADM 104, Naval Medical Department, include details of next-of-kin. These registers list the marine's name and rank, and under the heading 'Disposal' some information on posting from the division to a ship or station.

Division	Date range	Catalogue reference(s)
Chatham Division	1830–1913	ADM 183/114 to ADM 183/120
Plymouth Division	1862–1920	ADM 184/43 to ADM 184/54
Portsmouth Division (marriages only)	1869–1881	ADM 185/69
Woolwich Division	1822–1869	ADM 81/23 to ADM 81/25
Royal Marine Artillery	1810–1853	ADM 193/9
Royal Marine Artillery	1866–1921	ADM 6/437

Casualties, 1893–1956

Royal Marine casualties for this period are listed alphabetically in ADM 242/7 to ADM 242/10, giving name, rank, number, ship's name, date and place of birth, cause of death, where buried (including plot number) and next-of-kin. Hospital admission and discharge registers for the 2nd General Hospital, during 1918, are held in MH 106/986 to MH 106/997. Original records are as yet unavailable. Details of casualties from earlier periods may be found in the records listed below:

Register	Date range	Catalogue reference(s)
Registers of deaths in ships	1893–1909	ADM 104/109
Registers of deaths in ships	1910–1956	ADM 104/110 to ADM 104/121
Indexes to registers	1893–1950	ADM 104/102 to ADM 104/108
Registers of deaths	1900–1914	ADM 104/122
Registers of deaths	1915–1941	ADM 104/123 to ADM 104/126
Registers of deaths of naval ratings (and marines)	1939–1948	ADM 104/127 to ADM 104/139
Registers of killed and wounded	1854–1929	ADM 104/144 to ADM 104/149
Indexes to registers of killed and wounded	1915–1929	ADM 104/140, ADM 104/141, ADM 104/142

Other record groups at the National Archives

The Royal Marines' position in the armed forces can be viewed by the novice genealogist, as somewhere between the navy and the army. However crude this statement appears, there is some truth in it when it comes to their records, as these will appear in both the ADM (Admiralty) and WO (War Office) series. The marines' link to the WO series extends beyond the 1755 reorganization under the Admiralty, notably with the formation of commandos in the Second World War. Volunteers from army regiments formed the first of these in 1940, with Royal Marines being released to form their units from 1942. The role became exclusively Royal Marine after 1946. The examples that follow can give the researcher an idea of the type of Royal Marine records that exist, and where in the WO series they could appear in the archives.

WO 32/1041 Royal Marine Division of the Expeditionary Force, 1942–3
WO 32/10415 Special Service Brigade, 1942–5
WO 32/10416 Commandos: reorganization, 1943–6

WO 32/10417 Distribution of and policy for upkeep of commandos, 1943

WO 32/10418 Future of combined operations headquarters, 1943–4

WO 32/10494 Headdress, 1942–5

WO 32/10930 Functions of the chief of combined operations, 1944–6

WO 32/11539 34 Amphibian Support Regiments, Royal Marines – plans for the future, 1945–7

WO 106/4158 Commandos and Special Air Services Troops, June 1943–June 1945

WO 208/1262 Infantry: commandos and special tactical units, Dec. 1942–June 1945

WO 199/1763 Liaison with commandos and employment of, in the event of a raid, Nov. 1941–June 1943

WO 201/2152 Captured enemy report: enemy appraisal of British commandos, Mar. 1943

WO 199/1493 Royal Marines and War Office directly controlled static units: operational role, Mar. 1941–Mar. 1942

WO 199/680 Reorganization: Royal Marines, July 1943–1945

WO 373/88/1 Army awards to Royal Marines, Meritorious Service Awards: 5 Mar. 1942–2 July 1946

WO 106/5023 No.203 Military Mission: South African volunteers for the Royal Marines, Nov. 1942–Mar. 1944

For the same period the following examples are taken from a sub-series of ADM 1 and ADM 116:

ADM 1/13185 Royal Marines – General Matters (60): Army and Royal Marine Commandos: organization into Special Service Group

ADM 116/5306 Royal Marine Engineers: participation in Mobile Naval Base Defence Organization, 1940–5

ADM 1/15301 Armaments (11): Mobile Naval Base Defence Organization: reorganization and substitution of coast defence guns by anti-aircraft guns; RM Groups, MNBDO and additional heavy anti-aircraft batteries 1943

At a more personal level, some interesting transfers are recorded in the WO 97 series, a sample of which is listed below:

WO 97/63/98 JOSEPH HENRY Born LEEDS, Yorkshire. Served in 18th Dragoons (Light); 4th Dragoons; Royal Marines. Discharged aged 38, 1807–28

WO 97/64/15 CHARLES HERITAGE Born FROME, Somerset. Served in 2nd Dragoon Guards; Royal Marines. Discharged aged 36, 1807–26

WO 97/65/64 HENRY HIND Born LIVERPOOL, Lancashire. Served in 15th Dragoons (Light); 85th Foot Regiment; Royal Marines Plymouth. Discharged aged [not known], covering date gives year of enlistment, 1813

WO 97/67/73 THOMAS HOPKINS Born RANCE, Northamptonshire. Served in 2nd Dragoon Guards; Royal Marines. Discharged aged 42, 1807–32

WO 97/74/112 GEORGE JOYCE Born FROME, Somerset. Served in 7th Dragoons; Royal Marines. Discharged aged 26, 1804–18

The formation and development of the Ministry of Defence (MOD) between 1964 and 1971 leads to one further record group to consider. With the amalgamation of the Admiralty, War Office, Air Ministry and Ministry of Aviation, records of this period can appear in the DEFE series, for example:

DEFE 69/431 Bukit Timah Old Christian Cemetery, Singapore: installation of plaque and Book of Remembrance for Royal Navy and Royal Marines personnel buried between 1865 and 1907, 1 Jan. –31 Dec. 1965

DEFE 69/249 Operation BASCOTE (provision of Royal Marines aboard Naval Armament Vessel THROSK), 1 Jan. 1968–31 Dec. 1971

DEFE 69/427 The Loyal Toast: privilege to remain seated applied to Senior Ratings' and Royal Marines' messes, 1 Jan. 1964–31 Dec. 1977

Royal Marines service documents in the archive of the Fleet Air Arm Museum
The Fleet Air Arm Museum (FAAM) at the Royal Naval Air Station, Yeovilton, Somerset, assumed custody of a large number of service documents from the Ministry of Defence (navy records) in the 1990s. The quantity was such that the RM Museum did not have the space to house them, and so it acknowledges with thanks the care and work of the FAAM in saving these records from destruction. The authors are indebted to Captain Roy Swales RN for much of the work in bringing these records to an accessible status, and providing a description of their content.

The majority of records are those of non-commissioned personnel who enlisted in the Royal Navy and Royal Marines before about 1925. Also included are the papers of most of the men who were enlisted in the Corps for short service HO during the First World War. The Royal Marines records that are of particular interest for this book include the following:

Royal Marines Light Infantry (RMLI)
1. Plymouth Division continuous service – service numbers Plymouth/1 to Plymouth/23000.

2. Plymouth Division short service – service numbers Plymouth/1(S) to Plymouth/3300(S).
3. Chatham Division continuous service – service numbers Chatham/1 to Chatham/25000.
4. Chatham Division short service – service numbers Chatham 1(S) to Chatham/3500(S).
5. Portsmouth Division continuous service – service numbers Portsmouth/5500 to Portsmouth/23000.

The Portsmouth Division RMLI (CS) papers are mainly (but not exclusively) of those men who re-enlisted for pension (twenty-one years). Many other papers (for example of men who left after twelve years) have been separated from the main run of papers and are in the National Archives along with papers for Portsmouth Division short service (SS).

Royal Marine Artillery (RMA)

1. RMA continuous service – service numbers RMA/10000 to RMA/17200.
   Following the amalgamation of RMLI and RMA in 1923, these papers reflect the transfer of RMA men to Portsmouth Division numbers. The Portsmouth numbers use the original RMA numbers but were made into six-figure numbers by adding the prefix '2'. The RMA (CS) papers are mainly (but not exclusively) of those men who re-enlisted for pension (twenty-one years). As with the Portsmouth Division RMLI papers, many other papers (for example of men who left after twelve years) have been separated from the main run of papers and are in the National Archives. The papers of many other former RMA men may be found in the papers of the Chatham and Plymouth Divisions to which they transferred.

2. RMA short service – service numbers RMA/1(S) to RMA/3900(S).
   The papers of some RMA (SS) men, including most of those who were discharged dead (including killed in action) have, as mentioned above, been separated from the main run of papers and are at the National Archives, where they are mixed up with other Portsmouth/RMA papers.
   Royal Naval Division (Divisional Engineers, Divisional Train, RM Medical Unit and Ordnance Company) Deal short service – service numbers Deal/1(S) to Deal/4600(S).
   In addition to service papers, there are also RND record cards for most of these men.
   Royal Naval School of Music continuous service – service numbers RMB/1 to RMB/3100.

Royal Marines Labour Corps (RMLC) (New) short service – service numbers Deal/1N to Deal/1400N.

Royal Marines service papers
Records for an individual (sometimes referred to as Attestation Packs) were loose-filed in bundles or boxes in order of service number. They may contain an extensive record of a man's service from attestation to discharge, with a wealth of data in between. A description of the type of information contained in many of the RM records is presented below to give a feel for what may be available. An individual's papers might include:

- Original RM Attestation
- Army attestation of those who were conscripted or transferred
- Letters of release and recommendations from civilian employers
- Appeals against conscription
- Original arithmetic, handwriting and dictation tests
- Examination questions and worked answers for RM gunner
- Records of medical examination on entry and during service
- Active Service Casualty Forms (Army Forms B.103)
- RND Record Cards. Very few cards of RMLI men serving in the RND are in the main RND card index at the FAAM (see below)
- Conduct Record sheets – often for a whole career and with extensive lists of offences
- Various discharge papers, including parchment discharge certificates of those with previous service
- Invaliding Medical Record
- Hurt Certificate
- Report of accidental wounding
- Report of death in action
- Service certificates
- National Health insurance card
- Declaration of alias
- Court paternity orders and other court papers
- Correspondence to/from military authorities, including letters from next-of-kin
- Records of enquiries conducted in the field, often including original witness statements written in field notebooks
- First World War ration book
- Unemployment stamp book
- Active service will
- List of effects at death

- Naval pay book. The records of the many pensioners recalled for service on the outbreak of the Second World War usually retain their pay book, with photograph
- Army pay book from previous army service – some have been found to contain army identification discs (dog-tags).

The above list is by no means exhaustive. The documents as a whole give a remarkable overview of military life and contemporary society in the first decades of the twentieth century. Those of individuals can give an amazingly detailed record of their service in the Royal Marines. The amount of detail in the records held shows how comprehensive the RM records were and how destructive the administrative 'weeding' of certain records held at the National Archives has been. Even amongst the FAAM records there is evidence of this destructive process: the Conduct Record sheets had been removed from the Plymouth Division CS records. Fortunately, these were boxed separately and survived. The museum has now completed the task of sorting them and they will soon be reunited with the parent files. Inevitably there are gaps where records are (or appear to be) missing. Many of these may reflect inter-division, or inter-service transfers. It is known, however, that the papers of many men who had completed their twelve-year limited engagement and were recalled during the First World War from the Royal Fleet Reserve (RFR) are often absent. The whereabouts of these RFR papers is unknown.

Those with an interest in the Royal Marines will be drawn naturally to the records of service in the RMLI and/or RMA. However, the other records are important because they often contain information on parts of a man's service career outside the Royal Marines. For example, although most RNVR volunteers during the First World War found themselves serving as naval ratings with the Mediterranean Expeditionary Force (MEF) or British Expeditionary Force (BEF) as part of the Royal Naval Division (RND), many ratings were transferred to the RM to serve in units in the RND such as the Divisional Train, Ordnance Company or as RM Cyclists. Men who enlisted in the RMLI often transferred later to the Royal Navy and continued their service as, for example, stokers or ship's police. Of particular interest to the FAAM are those Royal Marines and naval ratings who moved across to the Royal Naval Air Service (RNAS) in the very early days of naval aviation. Some of these men were involved in the building of the first British rigid airship, the Admiralty's R.1 (also known as *MAYFLY*), in 1911. Some were commissioned as RNAS pilots and observers. Many of these ex-marines of the RNAS transferred to the fledgling Royal Air Force in 1918, some as aircraft mechanics, some in supporting trades. Even within the Royal Marines transfers were commonplace. Some RMLI men served in all three divisions, often more than once, and others moved to and from the Royal Naval School of Music and the RMA.

It is regrettable that the dispersion of records from the former MOD repository at Hayes has resulted in some RM records (including some Portsmouth CS, all Portsmouth SS and many RMA and RMLC) being stored in the National Archives at Kew. It is also known that there are many examples of papers at Kew being misfiled, RMA and RMLI records being mixed together. The Portsmouth Division papers at Kew appear to have suffered at some stage from drastic culling, and the papers are, unhelpfully for the researcher, filed by year of discharge and surname. There appears to be no clear justification for this splitting of the RM records, which will merely serve to complicate the work of the researcher.

Royal Naval Division Record Cards
The originals of the RND Record Cards have now also been transferred to the FAAM archive. The microfiche version is still available in the National Archives at Kew under ADM/339 (and is now available online) but this version contains numerous filing errors and some cards have not been copied correctly. It should also be noted that RND Record Cards for the Divisional Engineers, Divisional Train, RM Medical Unit and Ordnance Company held at the FAAM are not available in any form in the National Archives.

Indexes of First World War ships
Of Royal Marines interest are the indexes of First World War ships, depots and bases including trawlers and defensively armed merchant ships (DAMS) (1912–19 approx). Many Royal Marines, Royal Fleet Reservists and pensioners with prior sea service were recalled in 1914 to serve aboard these ships as gun crews for 3inch and 4inch destroyer guns that were mounted to deter surface-attacking U-boats. Royal Marines assigned to this duty often had the accounting base *President III* listed as their ship on their service record.

Current status
A continuing programme of work is under way to ensure that the many hundreds of thousands of papers (the RMLI Continuous Service papers alone cover some 63,000 service numbers) are properly cared for and indexed, but this is a very long-term effort and much still remains to be done. Indexing allows the papers to be searched either by surname or service number, but other data is now being recorded such as date of enlistment, date and place of birth and cause of discharge. Conservation and indexing has been completed for Chatham and RM Band CS, Plymouth, Chatham and RMA SS, as well as the Deal SS men of the RND (for whom a separate RND Record Card archive

has been formed). Work on Plymouth and Portsmouth CS and RMA CS is currently in progress.

4.5.3 *Diaries*

Personal diaries are often the most interesting unofficial document to be found in an archive, and if the author is the subject of the research, then this can be as good as it can get. However, a diarist of the same unit, or in the same operation or ship can be just as desirable. The diaries of Royal Marines at sea often focus on daily accounts of the weather and number of miles sailed between destinations, but occasionally an action or incident will feature that will warrant a more excited form of writing. In contrast, those written from the Western Front in 1916 can be short and grim, although the writers also mention food, letters and any small thing that either amuses them or lifts their spirits.

Diaries of Royal Marines are often retained by the families, and are often donated to museums or record offices only when the last close next-of-kin has been reached; however, copies or typescripts can enable the researcher to access the material. The RM Museum has, to date, 483 diaries of officers and men with a date range from 1776 to 1982. Diaries, when they are donated, can be offered to the most local record office or museum, and while some will be directed on to the RM Museum or Imperial War Museum, it is worth checking other collections such as the National Army Museum at Chelsea and the National Maritime Museum at Greenwich.

4.5.4 *Correspondence: individual and official*

The letters of individual Royal Marines within the collection of the RM Museum are housed in the Arch 11/12 series within date spans, but those written from an operational theatre, or that have specific content to an operation, will be found in the Arch 7/2–21 series, depending on date. Those letters and postcards written to and from prisoner of war camps will be found in the Arch 15/15 series, with separations according to date of conflict and location.

Official letters begin to be retained and organized during the eighteenth century, when a formal system of communication was established whereby correspondence between the Admiralty and each of the marine divisions would be copied by clerks into bound ledgers, and in turn the divisions would mirror the process for their communications to the Admiralty. This became known as the Admiralty in-and-out letter books; the Admiralty ones are mentioned in 4.5.2 under the ADM 191 series at the National Archives. Volumes of the marine divisions' letters to the Admiralty exist at the RM Museum Archive (Arch 2/7/2–7), the date range of these being 1755 to 1830.

The RM Museum Archive will include many official letters after this date in the form of divisional, unit, and headquarters registry files: these are the working files of correspondence relating to specific subjects such as administration, uniform changes, unit reorganization, ceremonial events and so forth.

4.6 Churches, cemeteries and memorials

Churches are a familiar point of reference for any genealogist since, quite apart from their religious practice, they represent a community and its records. Royal Marines and their families will feature in recorded christenings,

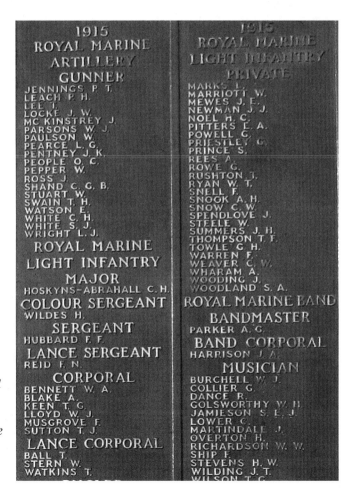

Some of the names on the Royal Navy Memorial Portsmouth of marines who died at sea in 1915, listed by rank for each branch of the Corps: RMA, RMLI and Band Service.

Ornate grave of Private Alfred Boulton RMLI of HMS Victor Emmanuel, *who died at Hong Kong on 16 October 1894.*

marriages, deaths and funerals. They can appear on memorial plaques, or sponsor the stained glass or pews that make up the actual fabric of the building. Their gravestones can be listed in the burial register. Church and parish records will normally be kept in town or county record offices and should feature on any researcher's list of places to check. Also remember that each RM barracks had its own church.

Many local history groups and societies tend to produce booklets of graves in their churches, and these are useful to the researcher who is out of area. Titles like *Service Graves in Portsmouth & Surrounding Area* by Staunton Park Genealogy Centre or *Royal Marines in Foreign Fields* by Brian Tarpey, listing graves on the island of Malta, can assist greatly. The *National Roll of the Great War* with volumes published by town or area was subject to next-of-kin supplying details, so it can be incomplete. Nevertheless, the information provided is sometimes fuller than an official notice of death. The naval war memorials of the home ports will not only list names but also have registers, while the RM divisions had books of remembrance at their respective barracks.

Outside periods of conflicts, a ship's company would often put up a memorial for comrades who died on voyage, while named graves can appear in the cemeteries of overseas bases such as Gibraltar, Hong Kong, San Juan and Ascension Islands. *The Cemetery Register for Singapore 1948–75* in two volumes is useful for researchers of this area as it relates to removal of Ulu Pandan and Pasir Panjang Military Cemeteries and the reburial at Kranji. *The Dead of the British Commonwealth West Malaysia 1948–1971* is another useful source; both are available at the RM Museum archive (Arch 17/8/4).

By far the largest single keeper of records of those British and Commonwealth service personnel killed in wars is the Commonwealth War Graves Commission. It was founded by Fabian Ware, the commander of a mobile unit of the British Red Cross, who felt compelled to establish a system to ensure the final resting places of casualties would not be lost for ever. Under his leadership, the mobile unit began recording and caring for all the graves they could find supported by a records department. Their work was given official recognition by the War Office, and relieved of their Red Cross duties, the unit was incorporated into the British Army as the Graves Registration Commission.

In May 1917, the Imperial War Graves Commission was established by Royal Charter, with the Prince of Wales serving as President and Ware as Vice-Chairman. With the work continuing beyond the Second World War, the commission is now responsible for recording 1.7 million casualties, at 23,000 sites in 150 countries. Enquiries can be made via their website at www.cwgc.org.

4.7 Problem areas

One of the main threats to the researching of family history is the family itself. Divorce and second or

The more plain style of headstone used by the Commonwealth War Graves Commission. Marine Brian Patrick Brownlie died on war service, 25 March 1945, and is buried at Kranji war cemetery, Singapore.

third marriages can consign the paper trail of the ex-marine into far corners of 'step-kin', or literally up in the smoke of an aggrieved party's bonfire! Far from this form of drama, sheer disinterest by one part of the family can have similar results, with the relics of 'old Dad' being thrown out with his eccentric collection of carrier bags.

Once engaged in the quest, some details that researchers may discover about a hitherto respected ancestor may well not be to their liking. Colonel Brian Edwards, when writing for the RM Historical Society's journal, *The Sheet Anchor*, stated that 'Marines are, and were, not saints, discipline was at times arbitrary and the temptations of exotic climes were real; gaol was a frequent resting place and throughout much of the nineteenth century officers were prone to find themselves in debtors' prison. Recollections of the old soldier can be transient and tales of "derring do" can grow with the passage of time – a simple gilding of the lily – while the opportunity to add a bar or two to a medal, or even a medal itself, could be seen as part of the simple process of keeping up with the Joneses or rejection of the system of entitlement.'

The opposite can also be true; many a 'would be' family historian is thwarted by a relative who 'would never talk about it', for example. Again, oral history – or testimony, as it should be called – should not be relied on for fact, since that is not its purpose. The fashion for 'experience' in a socio-historical context is often at odds with the military subjects being interviewed, who are usually of a generation who check and correct their contribution with fact and modesty to make it acceptable to themselves. Conversely, there is also some truth in the saying 'never let the obstacle of fact hinder the progress of a good yarn', but it is not exclusively the ancestral subject that can contribute to the family mythology. Some family historians seek to place their research into a preconceived context that they and others understand, by assumed linkage to a known event or famous person. Hence the combined weight of ancestors, who are claimed to have been aboard HMS *Victory* with Lord Nelson at the Battle of Trafalgar in 1805, would have sunk the ship without the otherwise necessary attentions of the French. Likewise, not all Victorian Royal Marines would have heard of Charles Dickens or have owned a horse and carriage.

Perhaps the most frustrating problem to the researcher is the 'missing record', the incidence where a record has been listed as existing but cannot be found. Around three and a half million service records and other records of the First World War were destroyed in September 1940 when a German bombing raid struck the War Office repository in Arnside Street, London. Fire and flood has been another cause of destruction in record repositories. Often it is the move to digitization and surrogate copies of sources that reduces the risk of the effects of this form of disaster.

Death can be another problem, not so much in its occurrence, which in terms of record keeping is usually a good traceable thing, but more in 'how?'. This is especially true when tracing material of a Royal Marine who has no known grave or who is buried at sea, who may be commemorated on a memorial, but that little else appears obvious. The loss of a marine in a ship sunk at sea has a sense of conclusion, but an unfound body in a land operation leads to many more questions. 'Missing presumed killed' will inevitably cause the researcher to trace records, evidence, witnesses even, to understand what happened. The answers are not always forthcoming: the destruction of war can often be the total destruction of a person; all that remains is an assumption.

The occurrence of shellshock and combat stress are more readily talked of in this current century than the two preceding ones, where reference to it usually appears only as a one-line cause for discharge or, at worst, being regarded with an attitude of cowardice. A Chatham Division discharge list of 1795 had a questionable entry when it recorded 'urinary incontinence due to service' against a number of names; a young First World War officer had a commission terminated with 'LMF' (lacking moral fibre) as the cause. The term 'insanity' appears often on sick and discharge lists in the nineteenth century, but psychiatric problems could be disguised in the following century with the term 'PURMS' (permanently unfit for Royal Marines service). Finding a paper trail in these types of medical situations can be frustrating.

Desertion is another area where the act will be recorded along with any subsequent arrest and punishment process. However, the letter 'R' (run) being entered on the service document does not give the answers to what happened or why, if the man is not recaptured. Motives for desertion usually have the common thread of seeking to improve one's situation; some have a criminal intent such as fraudulent enlistment. The recruit would enlist in a regiment and claim the bounty pay, then desert and join another regiment under another name, collecting another bounty. The book *Ships' Deserters 1852-1900* by Jim Melton (Library of Australian History 1986) lists 10,000 notified names of seamen (merchant, naval, and some Royal Marines) who deserted their ships when reaching Australia and hearing of the discovery of gold in 1851.

The serious researcher should always be open to the possibilities of the service life of an ancestor; fact and proof may not always be available to determine truth. Finally, experience suggests that successful research depends on a combination of diligent effort, persistence and good luck. It is hoped that guides such as this book and the various online catalogues that are beginning to appear will help the Royal Marine genealogist get started and make sense of some of the material that comes to light. The information may help to identify other more complex avenues to explore. The skills acquired in these processes will then help to recognize when diminishing returns make it sensible to stop.

Appendix 1

CODED FORMS

The following list is a selection of coded forms that will provide details relating to a Royal Marine's service. Some may be of the type inherited by the family, others will possibly be in the archives and repositories described in this work.

B334	Life Pensioner recall (1906–)
GH Form 35	Certificate of entry to Royal Hospital School, Greenwich
M22	Patient Discharge Certificate (Royal Naval Hospitals)
M183	Certificate for Wounds & Hurts
R105	Document of Attestation
R110	Particulars of Service upon discharge from the Royal Marines
R111	Certificate of Discharge, Royal Marines (revised 1917 and 1935)
R111a	Character Certificate on Demobilization (est. 1917; revised 1955)
R131	Muster roll for embarkation to service afloat
R133a	Drill and Musical History Sheet (Royal Marines Band)
R138	Certificate of Service (S535 & S-1241) (revised 1918 and 1939)
R154	Company Conduct Sheet
R165	Copy of Attestation to serve in the Royal Marines for twelve years (1914)
R274	Detachment Record Book of service afloat. Gives full information of mustered men for any given ship
R292	RM Certificate of Education (revised 1928)
R379	RM Swimming Certificate (revised 1913)

R380	RM Certificate of Qualification (trade, skill, etc.) (est. 1894; revised 1927)
R381	Certificate of Qualification for Promotion
R382	Permanent Divisional Pass 1894–
S367	Declaration to be made by a marine renewing his service
S369	Request for furlough on paying off (ship's detachment)
S332a	Report of Survey on Men (Royal Naval Hospitals)
S1586(A)	Order of release from Naval Service Class A
S1039	Pay list form
S1072a	Local information affecting pay and allowances (used by COPRA: see Appendix 2)
S1306	Protection and Identity Certificate (est. 1918)

Appendix 2

ABBREVIATIONS

The following is a selected list of abbreviations and phrases from various periods frequently found on coded documents such as R23, R138, S535 and S1241.

Act. or A/	prefix for temporary rank
AWOL	absent without leave
Bdr.	bombardier, junior non-commissioned rank Royal Marine Artillery 1804–1923
Bd./Cpl.	band corporal
Bd./Sgt.	band sergeant
BEF	British Expeditionary Force
CCAC	Commando Cliff Assault Centre
CELLS	confined to ships' cells or barracks detention block
CH/	service number prefix for Chatham Division
CHU	Commando Holding Unit
CM	courts martial
CMWTC	Commando Mountain Warfare Training Centre
COPRA	Combined Operations Pay and Records Administration (including RM landing craft crews 1939–46)
Cpl.	corporal
C/Sgt	colour sergeant (sometimes Col-Sgt)
CSM	company sergeant-major
DAMS	Defensively Armed Merchant Ships (1914–18)

DD	discharged dead (usually written in red pencil or heavy black ink)
Demob.	Demobilization followed by release class and date
DEMS	Defensively Equipped Merchant Ships (1939–45)
DEPOT	Deal
D/Maj.	drum major
DWS	died on war service (as opposed to KIA)
EX/	service number prefix for Exton 1939–42
FP	field punishment, usually followed by a number that would refer to a set discipline tabled in King/Queen's Regulations, and with days forfeited
GD	general duties
HBL	home base ledger (personnel within the UK)
HDML	Harbour Defence Motor Launch
Hd.Qtrs	headquarters (usually followed by division)
H.O.	Hostilities Only (1939–46)
I of M	instructor of musketry
ITC	Infantry Training Centre (also CTCRM, Lympstone, Exton, etc.)
JSAWC	Joint Services Amphibious Warfare Centre
K.I.A.	killed in action
L/Cpl.	lance corporal (also L/Sgt.)
LS&GC	Long Service & Good Conduct Medal
MCTC	Military Correction Training Centre
MEF	Mediterranean Expeditionary Force (1915–16)
M.I.A.	missing in action
MID	mentioned in despatches
MNBDO	Mobile Naval Base Defence Organization
Mne.	marine, entry rank of Royal Marines from 1923 onwards
MOA	Marine Officer's Attendant
MSM	Meritorious Service Medal (can be with annuity)
NCO	non-commissioned officer
NGSM	Naval General Service Medal

NP	naval party
NSSC	Novice Ski and Survival Course (Arctic Warfare Qualification)
'On Passage'	aboard ship or transport but not part of detachment
PLY	service number prefix for Plymouth Division
PO	service number prefix for Portsmouth Division
POW	prisoner of war
Pte.	private, entry rank of marines up to 1923
PURMS	permanently unfit for Royal Marines service
PWC	postwar clothing (1939–45)
R	run, deserted
RFR	Royal Fleet Reserve (*c.* 1900–14) sometimes given as a number prefix
RMA	service number prefix for Royal Marine Artillery up to 1923
RMB	Royal Marine barracks
RMB	as service number prefix for Royal Marine Band personnel
RME	Royal Marine Engineers (1939–46)
RMG	Recommended for Medal and Gratuity (see NGSM & MSM)
RMLC	Royal Marine Labour Corps (1917–19)
RMLI	Royal Marines Light Infantry (1855–1923)
RMP	Royal Marine Police (1922–49); also RMPSR Special Reserve
RMRD	Royal Marine Reserve Depot
RMSM	Royal Marine School of Music
RMTG	Royal Marines Training Group (*c.* 1942–6) usually one of four camps, in Wales
RNAS	Royal Naval Air Service 1914–18
RND	Royal Naval Division (1914–18) RM provided two battalions and support units. Sometimes referred to as Victory Brigade and RM Brigade 1914–15

RNSM	Royal Naval School of Music (1903–50) (s) indicating short service when placed after service number (1914–18)
RR	recommended for re-engagement
SEAC	South East Asia Command (1942–6)
Sgt.	sergeant
SOS	struck off strength
Sup. or Supy.	supernumerary, attached but not on the strength of i.e. unit or ship
TG	training group (see RMTG)
TOS	taken on strength
Tpy. or Tempy.	temporary rank or appointment
TSM	troop sergeant-major
TTD	Technical Training Department (Fort Cumberland, Portsmouth *c.* 1926–1973)
WAR CHEVRONS	sometimes known as service stripes, worn point up on lower right sleeve
WG	war gratuity
WO	warrant officer
WOUND STRIPES	two inch lengths of gold or red braid worn above left sleeve cuff. Issued for each time wounded
WSI	war service increment paid for years of war service completed 1939–45

FURTHER READING

There are any numbers of books describing different aspects of the Royal Marines. Those below include some of the more useful. Brooks, Ladd and Thompson have extensive bibliographies. Publishers are London unless shown otherwise.

Ambler, John, *The Royal Marines Band Service* (Royal Marines Historical Society 2003)

Blumberg, H E, *Britain's Sea Soldiers: A Record of the Royal Marines during the War 1914–1919* (Swiss, Devonport 1927; reprinted Naval and Military Press, Uckfield 2007)

Brooks, R E, *The Long Arm of Empire: Naval Brigades from the Crimea to the Boxer Rebellion* (Constable 1999)

———, *The Royal Marines: 1664 to the Present* (Constable 2002)

Brown, George A, *Commando Gallantry Awards of WWII* (London Stamp Exchange: 1991)

Clowes, W Laird, *The Royal Navy: A History from the Earliest Times*, vols 3–7 (repr. Chatham Publishing 1997)

Connolly, S, *Spink's Guide to the Wearing of Orders, Decorations, and Medals* (Spink & Son 1986)

Douglas-Morris, K J, *Naval Medals 1793–1856* (Douglas-Morris 1987)

———, *Naval Medals 1856-1880* (Naval and Military Press, Uckfield 1996)

———, *The Naval Long Service Medals* (A Rowe, Eastbourne 2002)

Edye, L, *Historical Records of the Royal Marines, etc.*. vol. 1 (Harrison 1893)

Fevyer, W H and and J W Wilson, *The 1914 Star to the Royal Navy and Royal Marines* (Naval and Military Press, Uckfield 1995)

Field, C, *Britain's Sea Soldiers*, vols 1 and 2 (Lyceum Press, Liverpool 1924)

Fletcher, D, *War Cars: British Armoured Cars in the First World War* (HMSO 1987)

Fraser, E and L G Carr-Laughton, *The Royal Marine Artillery* (RUSI 1930) vols 1 and 2

Good, J A, *With Full and Grateful Hearts: A Register of Royal Marines War Deaths 1914–1919* (Royal Marines Museum, Eastney 1991)

———, *Bid Them Rest in Peace: A Register of Royal Marines War Deaths 1939–1945* (Royal Marines Museum, Eastney 1992)

Griffin, P D, *Encyclopaedia of Modern British Army Regiments* (Sutton, Stroud 2006)

Hill, R, *The Prizes of War: The Naval Prize System in the Napoleonic Wars 1793–1815* (Sutton, Stroud and RN Museum, Portsmouth 1998)

Houlding, J A, *Fit For Service: The Training of the British Army 1715–1795* (Oxford: Oxford University Press, 1981)

Jerrold, D, *The Royal Naval Division* (repr. Naval and Military Press, Uckfield *c.* 2000)

Kipling, A L and H L King, *Head Dress Badges of the British Army*: vol. 1, *Up to the End of the Great War* (Muller 1978); vol. 2: *From the End of the Great War to the Present Day* (Muller 1979)

Ladd, J D, *By Sea, By Land: The Royal Marines 1919–1997* (HarperCollins 1998)

Lavery, B, *Shipboard Life and Organisation 1731–1815* (Navy Records Society 1998)

Little, M G, *The Royal Marines and the Victoria Cross* (Royal Marines Museum, Eastney, 2002)

Lowe, J A, *Records of the Portsmouth Division of Marines 1764–1800* (City of Portsmouth 1990)

May, W E, W Y Carman and J Tanner, *Badges and Insignia of the British Armed Services* (A&C Black 1974)

Moulton, J L, *The Royal Marines* (Leo Cooper 1972; revised 1981)

National Archive, *Guide to the Contents of the Public Record Office*, 3 vols (HMSO 1963)

Pappalardo, B, *Tracing Your RN Ancestry* (The National Archive 2003)

Pitkin, *The Royal Marines* (Pitkin Pictorial 1971)

Rodger, N A M, *The Command of the Ocean: A Naval History of Britain 1649–1815* (Allen Lane 2004)

Royal Marine Historical Society, *A Short History of the Royal Marines 1664–2004* (RMHS, Portsmouth 2004)

Spencer, W, *Medals: The Researcher's Guide* (The National Archive 2006)

Stadden, C and G and C Newark, *Uniforms of the Royal Marines 1664 to the Present* (The Pompadour Gallery, 1997)

Thomas, G, *Records of the Royal Marines* (PRO Publications 1994)

Thompson, J, *The Royal Marines: From Sea Soldiers to a Special Force* (Sidgwick & Jackson 2000)

Wall, P H B and G A M Ritson, *The Royal Marine Pocket Book*: Part 2, *Organisation* (Gale and Polden, Aldershot 1945)